ONE IN A SERIES FROM THE PUBLISHERS OF *PRE-K TODAY*

LEARNING THROUGH PLAY

BLOCKS

A Practical Guide for Teaching Young Children

Written by Ellen Booth Church *and* Karen Miller

·

Foreword by Barbara Day

Published by:
Scholastic Inc.
Early Childhood Division
730 Broadway
New York, NY 10003

12, 11, 10, 9, 8, 7, 6, 5, 4, 3   3, 4, 5, 6, 7/9
                                                          33

Printed in the U.S.A.

ISBN # 0-590-49111-3
Library of Congress Catalog Number

CONTENTS

LEARNING AND GROWING WITH BLOCKS

PAGE 7

PLANNING FOR PLAY IN THE BLOCK AREA

PAGE 25

ACTIVITY PLANS
FOR TWOS, THREES, FOURS, AND FIVES

PAGE 35

COVER PHOTO: JAMES LEVIN

BLOCK CITY

What are you able to
 build with your blocks?
Castles and palaces,
 temples and docks.
Rain may keep raining,
 and others go roam,
Let the sofa be mountains,
 the carpet be sea,
There I'll establish a city for me . . .

By Robert Louis Stevenson

FOREWORD
A Conversation With Barbara Day About the Value of Block Play

Q: **Why is block play important?**

A: Play with blocks provides the foundation for learning in every area of a child's development. It offers children joy, challenge, visual stimulation, and tactile stimulation through a variety of creative learning activities with blocks. To build, change, and build again at will develops a sense of mastery, and growing mastery gives children joy in their accomplishments.

The expressive and developmental opportunities offered by blocks are almost limitless. Block play engages the whole child in creative and multidimensional physical, social, emotional, artistic, and cognitive endeavors.

Q: **Can children of all developmental levels benefit from block play?**

A: Yes, definitely. Block play is attractive and pleasurable to children from infancy onward. Blocks are easily adaptable to children's individual developmental levels, learning styles, and to their interests and needs. Two-year-olds can know the gratification of success in creating stacks of blocks, just as five-year-olds can enjoy building complex structures.

An individualized medium for learning, blocks offer opportunities for exploration and mastery at any level.

Q: **Which developmental areas are developed through block play?**

A: Specifically, block play builds conceptual thinking in the areas of part/whole relationships, comparison of size and quantity, and shapes and numbers. Block play further contributes to cognitive development by developing sorting and classification skills, pattern recognition, empirical thinking, and problem-solving skills. Finally, block play promotes the development of eye-hand coordination, visual perception skills, large and small muscle control, as well as the aesthetic appreciation essential to all creative endeavors.

Q: **Does block play contribute to social and emotional development as well?**

A: As children engage in creative and dramatic block play they develop self-esteem and a sense of personal competence. It also provides for the healthy expression of feelings and ideas. Particularly in times of stress, older children will return to block play again and again. Block play provides a chance to regress and experience the feelings of competency and comfort associated with previously mastered skills.

Dramatic play with blocks allows for the role testing and exploration that is essential to the development of an authentic and healthy self-concept.

Block play also offers opportunities for sharing, communication, group problem-solving, and the development of sensitivity to the needs of others. As children play cooperatively, they are required to coordinate their desires and actions with the desires and actions of others.

Q: What is the adult's role in block play?

A: Recognizing the value of block play is probably the first step. The second is understanding how to provide an atmosphere that maximizes the experience for children. This involves letting the child take the active role and direct the play, while the adult takes on the more passive role of observer and assistant. Naturally, you may introduce an interesting accessory or ask a question that extends learning, but the adult's role is to support play, not to direct it.

Q: What can adults learn by observing children's play with blocks?

A: Valuable insights into children's development and their perceptions of themselves and the world can be gained from observing children at play with blocks. The symbolic representations children create during block play may be different even when they create something together. For example, two four-year-old boys in a preschool class cooperatively built a block structure. One boy's description of the structure is simply, "It's an office, just like the one my daddy works in." The other child spins an elaborate tale of a castle with turrets, a moat, and a drawbridge. While it's obvious that this structure represents something different to each boy, it also indicates that blocks are versatile and allow for open-ended play and interpretation.

By observing children's play, and asking questions without intruding, adults can gain valuable insight and information about what children are creating.

Q: How would you summarize the value of block play?

A: Block play provides children with both basic skills and creative outlets. Although the activities in this book are designed for children from two to five years of age, activities with blocks can be structured to provide engaging experiences for children of any age. Many of the skills in block play are prerequisites for later reading and math skills. In short, "building with blocks" is exactly what the name implies: *building materials for the child's total growth.*

Barbara Day is the author of Early Childhood Education: Creative Learning Activities, *Third Edition, Macmillan, and is professor and chair, Curriculum and Instruction, at the University of North Carolina at Chapel Hill. Dr. Day is a past president of the Association of Supervision and Curriculum Development (ASCD) and currently chairs ASCD's policy commission on early childhood education.*

LEARNING AND GROWING WITH BLOCKS

- **HOW CHILDREN GROW THROUGH BLOCK PLAY**
- **YOUR ROLE IN BLOCK PLAY**
- **LEARNING AND GROWING WITH BLOCKS: DEVELOPMENTAL CHART**
- **USING BLOCKS WITH CHILDREN WHO HAVE SPECIAL NEEDS**
- **TALKING TO PARENTS ABOUT BLOCK PLAY**
- **A MESSAGE TO PARENTS**

PHOTO: JAMES LEVIN

HOW CHILDREN GROW THROUGH
BLOCK PLAY

You need only to watch a child at play in the block area to be reminded of how delightful blocks can be. For the youngest child, blocks are a wondrous source of pleasure and discovery. As they stack block upon block, then tumble them down, they feel a sense of power and strength. As toddlers grasp and drop blocks during play, they enjoy the weight, feel, or the sound of the blocks when they fall.

For the older child, who works in painstaking fashion to create an elaborate structure, block play is exciting, inspiring, and greatly satisfying. As structures are built block upon block, they take on a life and story that interests and motivates the child. These structures may reflect a child's recent experience or adventure, a wildly imaginative idea, or an issue or event that may be of concern to him or her.

Whatever the motivation, it's the *process* of building and creating that is rewarding and important for the child. How often have we seen a child create a tower and, with a swift wave of the hand, knock it down? While we may wonder *why*, what we need to remember is that demolishing a building is part of the *process* of the child creating and elaborating on her own drama.

On the other hand, children sometimes like to keep their structures intact for a while. They feel a sense of accomplishment and pride as peers, teachers, or parents acknowledge their creations by commenting on and asking questions about them. Understanding and respecting children's play in the block area (and other areas as well), develops greater insight and appreciation for how children play and the process they experience.

LEARNING AND GROWING

During the day in a busy preschool, child-care program, family day-care home, or kindergarten classroom, it's easy to overlook children's play in the block area. However, if you take the time to observe and assist children during play you can help facilitate their development physically, socially, emotionally, creatively, and cognitively. Here are some specific ways that block play promotes a child's overall development and how curriculum areas such as math, language, science, art, and dramatic play are reinforced.

■ *Physically,* block play provides opportunities for the development of eye-

PHOTO: JAMES LEVIN

Two-year-olds may:

■ carry blocks around, learning how to hold onto them, how heavy they feel, and how they sound when they fall.

■ make a simple tower by stacking blocks unevenly, then joyfully knock it down.

■ lay blocks side-by-side on the floor.

■ build horizontally by placing blocks end-to-end.

Three-year-olds may:

■ construct enclosures in their structures that resemble rooms, pens, or yards.

■ make bridges by standing two blocks upright and placing a third block across the top.

■ begin to name their constructions, as they build or when describing a construction to someone else.

■ play alone or near other children, but rarely in a cooperative way.

hand coordination, perceptual and sensory-motor development, and large and small muscle control.

■ *Cognitively,* block play refines a range of intellectual skills.
• Mathematically, it reinforces readiness skills such as sorting and classifying, part/whole relationships, equivalencies, experience with shapes and patterns, and offers real-life use of number concepts and problem-solving.
• Language and vocabulary development are reinforced as children play with and describe their constructions.
• Finally, science processes and concepts, such as making predictions and comparisons, or experimenting with gravity, balance, and cause and effect, happen naturally as children interact with blocks.

■ *Socially,* block play offers opportunities for sharing, communicating, and cooperating. When children play together in the block area, even if they are engaging in parallel play, they must

consider available floor space, the number of blocks, and what other children want to build. When desires conflict, children can be helped to negotiate and compromise.

■ *Emotionally,* blocks provide a healthy outlet. Children can find comfort in the familiar activity of block building. Through dramatic play with blocks, they can assume powerful roles, explore emotions, and re-create day-to-day experiences. These are all essential to developing a healthy self-concept, especially if teachers and caregivers "tune in" by assisting with needed accessories, asking questions, and commenting to extend and enhance children's play.

■ *Creatively,* blocks inspire artistic expression while challenging children's imaginations and creative-thinking abilities. As they create, children decide where blocks and accessories will go to create interesting designs, patterns, or structures. They begin to develop an aesthetic awareness as they combine blocks in appealing ways.

The degree of physical, intellectual, social, and emotional development encouraged by block play depends on several factors. Two key ones are a child's developmental level and his experience with blocks. Children at different ages play with blocks in different ways. But even within an age group, individual children use blocks in a variety of ways. A three-year-old who has had a lot of exposure to blocks may build at a more complex level than a five-year-old who has rarely played with them.

On these pages are some very general guidelines that describe "typical" behaviors of children ages two, three, four, and five when playing with blocks. (See "Two-year-olds may...," "Three-year-olds may...," etc.) Use these as a guide when observing a particular child to determine his or her level of play. But remember that you are likely to observe a range of behaviors within each age group.

Four-year-olds may:

■ combine enclosures and bridges to make more complex buildings.

■ make a series of bridges.

■ use their block constructions as settings for dramatic play involving figures of people, animals, and cars.

■ recognize pattern and symmetry, and select blocks in order to continue an established pattern.

■ begin to share ideas, cooperate, and build with others.

Five-year-olds may:

■ plan systematically by deciding what they want to build, and to name the constructions, before they begin.

■ build elaborate structures that have pattern and symmetry, with details like ramps and doors.

■ build cooperatively with other children.

■ individually create buildings, then together use all of the structures in cooperative play.

■ with an adult's help, make written labels for buildings, describe them, or tell stories about them.

■ enjoy leaving buildings up and modifying them from day to day.

■ use crayons, clay, and other materials to add extra detail to structures.

YOUR ROLE
IN BLOCK PLAY

There are many factors that influence children's experience with blocks. Some of these are the number and variety of blocks and accessories to play with, the amount of time kids have to develop their ideas, and the degree of your interest and support. While all three are important, a key factor is your interest in block play. By effectively organizing the block area, facilitating social interactions, and looking for opportunities to extend children's thinking as they build, you'll send the message that you value their play. When children sense this, block play is a more gratifying and enriching experience for them. Here are some guidelines to consider.

■ *Organize and arrange the physical space.* Organizing for block play involves arranging the space and the materials. Young children learn by watching and interacting with other children, so there must be enough room for several children to play comfortably together. Materials should be easy for children to find. Accessory items should change from time to time to add variety and to renew children's interest. (See "Planning for Play in the Block Area," pages 25-34.)

■ *Allow children time to create.* Children need an uninterrupted span of time to develop their ideas. Ten or 15 minutes may be enough for two-year-olds, while 45 minutes to an hour is more satisfying for older children. Based on your daily schedule and children's needs, allow enough time so that your most enthusiastic builders can have a satisfying building experience.

■ *Acknowledge children's constructions in a meaningful way.* Self-esteem can develop from a child feeling that he or she has done something well and that others value the work. Therefore try to make praise meaningful. Rather than saying, "Oooh, I like that!" or "That's nice" about something a child builds, point out details that demonstrate your genuine interest. You can respond by saying, "Gee,...this is a really interesting building. Could you tell me about it?...Really? You know I think this house has even more rooms than the one you built yesterday. You used a lot of the smaller blocks to create this one, too."

When children are especially pleased with their constructions, give them a chance to relish in their accomplishments. If you have the space and they ask to leave their building up for the morning, you can give them a "do not disturb" sign to put on their structures. The presence of the sign says, "This building is important to me, please be careful."

■ *Follow the child's lead during play.* When interacting with children in the block area, it's important to remember that it's *their* play, *their* ideas, and *their* dramatic themes that are being created around blocks. Try to think of yourself as an assistant to the child — letting him or her direct the action, set the tone, and develop the drama. While you ask questions to clarify and enhance their play, observe and comment upon what is happening, and provide props and assistance when needed. This does not mean that you cannot make suggestions or introduce a play theme now and then, but that your ideas should be offered as *suggestions* rather than directions. Finding the right balance of adult participation is not always easy. However, if a child is directing the drama, initiating new twists, and giving directions to *you* on how you can "assist" or participate, then you are following the child's lead as a respectful play partner.

■ *Communicate the value of block play to parents.* Discussing children's block building with parents is a way to boost children's self-esteem and help parents understand its importance. You can tell parents what the child was saying while playing and the skills the child demonstrated in creating a particular construction. Having children's dictation on hand to show parents, or notes taken while you observed the child at play, will help parents understand how

meaningful the experience was for their child.

LEARN BY OBSERVING

One of the best ways to extend children's learning in the block area is by observing their play. Through your observations you can also gain valuable insight into children's interests, emotional ideas, creative thinking, problem-solving abilities, and social interactions. In turn, these observations can be used as a basis for interacting with children during play. For instance, if you observe that a child builds and crashes a structure over and over again, you can say, "I noticed that your building keeps falling down. What's happening to it?" Approaching a child this way, based on behavior you have observed, communicates that you share an interest in what the child is doing. It encourages the child to elaborate on his or her actions and ideas.

Keeping a notebook to briefly record activities and behaviors you observe is a good way to keep track of children's development throughout the year. This information is also valuable to share with parents. What should you look for? The following are some questions, areas to observe, and suggested ways to use these observations as a basis for approaching and interacting with your children.

FOSTER PRO-SOCIAL PLAY

In the block area, children often have the greatest difficulty in three areas of social interaction — joining a group, sharing and taking turns, and negotiating disputes. Often it helps to give children the words they need to communicate their ideas and feelings. Here are some guidelines to help children initiate and maintain positive social interactions.

Assist children in joining a group. When a child joins a group by barging in and knocking down someone's building or grabbing something, the child

BLOCK PLAY WITH MIXED-AGE GROUPS

If you're a family day-care provider, or a caregiver in a program with mixed-age groups, you have children of many different ages and developmental levels playing together. However, sometimes children of different ages don't always play peacefully together. If this is a concern in your program, here are a few suggestions to try:

■ Be observant. Remind children (especially younger ones) that they can only play with or knock over their own constructions — and not someone else's. Give this toddler his or her own blocks with which to build.

■ Anticipate and prevent mishaps. It can help to mark off certain sections on the floor with tape for each child's buildings. Make sure everyone can get to the blocks without walking over someone else's structure.

■ Acknowledge the needs of all children. Try using furniture to section off a "big kids' building area." Periodically schedule a special "toddler time" in the block area, while the older children engage in other activities — then switch.

■ Prevent situations where older children "take over." Help children understand that the block area is for everyone. Remind older children that they cannot exclude toddlers from playing. If a problem arises, they are to immediately notify an adult.

may be experiencing strong feelings that he or she cannot express easily. It may be helpful for you or an assistant to spend a few minutes helping the child work out these feelings. Then you can reintroduce her to the group. Here are some suggestions to try.

■ *Help the child find a way to add to the play going on.* "Christopher, I see you want to play with Keith and Jana. Keith and Jana, is it OK for Christopher to join you? Maybe you can tell him how he can help you." If this doesn't work, encourage parallel play and suggest the child position himself next to the others and build his own structure. Often interactions may occur naturally.

■ *Model language children can use to enter play.* "Martha, it makes Juan angry when you push him. If you want to play with him, ask, 'May I play?'"

Facilitate sharing and taking turns. Sharing and taking turns are *not* realistic expectations for caregivers of twos and young threes. Therefore the suggestions that follow are appropriate for older threes, fours, and fives.

■ *Help children use words to request a turn.* Rather than grabbing or hoarding blocks help children use phrases such as, "May I play with that when you're through?" or "I'll let you use it as soon as I'm finished." When a child is reluctant to share a popular item, explain that she may play with it for "a few more minutes," then should give it to the next child. Often children will give up a toy more quickly and willingly if they are given a little more time with it, rather than being ordered to relinquish the object immediately.

■ *Offer an interesting alternative to the child waiting for a turn with a toy.* "Kerry, can you use these dolls while you're waiting for the other ones?"

■ *If possible, encourage two children to find ways to use a toy together.* For example, one child could drive a toy car one way on a block "road" and the other child could drive it back.

Help negotiate disputes. Although it may be tempting to take over when kids are having verbal battles, work more to help children express themselves and be

OBSERVATION GUIDE

1. *What is the child doing with the blocks?* Depending upon the developmental level of the child, he or she may just load and unload blocks in a wagon, or be intent on creating a building. Maybe a child is using the blocks as props in play rather than using the blocks for building and dramatic play. In either case, describe the action or constructions, and anything the child may have been saying about her play.

2. *Does the child have the language to describe what he or she is making?* If a child has limited vocabulary, model language she might use by describing the building as you see it: "Jessica, I see you created a big building there. Let's see, you used the long blocks down here, and then pillars in the middle...." If a child seems interested, you can write down descriptions of the child's structure, then read the words aloud. This will help the child become more aware of language.

3. *Does a child seem to make the same things over and over?* Remember that a certain amount of repetition is fine, but if the same play theme continues over a long period of time, it may indicate that the child could use a little encouragement to elaborate further.

Relating block play to a theme can inspire builders to try new ideas. Put up theme-related pictures on the wall at floor level and add theme-related accessories to the material shelves. Special hats to wear while building can also add to the fun.

Be careful, though, not to give children the impression that they *must* make a certain type of structure. The block area is a place for children's ideas, even if the same ones seem to frequently appear.

4. *Can a child think of ways to solve problems, and will he or she try different solutions?* Try not to be too eager to step in and help with technical prob-

heard as they negotiate. There will be times when you will need to intervene and times when you'll want to give them a chance to try to settle their own disputes. Here are some suggestions.

■ *Remind children that everyone is welcome in the block area.* "You can't play here" is a hurtful phrase that should not be ignored. This is a time to intervene by reminding children that no one may be excluded from any play area if the area has not reached its maximum number of children. "Everyone can play here," is a quick, simple reminder.

■ *Help children understand that accidents are not intentional.* Sometimes you may need to step in to help a child recognize that an accident was not intentional. When a building falls, a child may become upset that his or her work has been ruined. Reassure and empathize with the victim: "I can see you're very unhappy about your building. I'm sure Jerry feels very sorry. He didn't mean to do it. It was an accident." Then help the child who caused the accident to express his feelings and explain how it happened. If it seems

likely, you might suggest that the children work together to rebuild the structure. This may help both feel better.

■ *Help children use words when conflicts arise.* Often children don't have the vocabulary to express how they feel, so often they react with physical aggression. This is the clearest way for them to communicate their anger. You can help by saying, "Max, I can't let you hit or push anyone. Use words to help Toby understand how you feel." When conflicts can be solved with different solutions, you can suggest alternatives for children to try. Finally, acknowledge children's independent solutions: "Great. You figured out a way to use the truck together."

When you are pretty sure that children possess the skills and words to solve minor disputes, try "discipline by proximity." When a conflict is brewing, simply sit down near the children and look interested. Often they will remember how to negotiate properly. Be sure to comment on positive results: "Good thinking! I knew you two could work this out."

lems, such as how to balance blocks or prevent a structure from falling. Trial and error is an important part of learning. But if a child seems frustrated or is giving up, then it may be time to assist.

First, ask the child to describe the problem. Then respond, "I noticed you tried a couple of things. What else do you think might work? OK, why don't you try that." Even if it still doesn't work, the child feels reassured by your presence — and senses that you're "in this together."

Finally you can suggest a solution or two, giving the child an opportunity to make a choice. "Sometimes if you place the larger blocks on the bottom, and smaller ones on top, the tower will stand. Or you can...." This allows the child to experiment, still solving the problem independently.

5. *What new concepts, discoveries, or developmental abilities has a child mastered?* It's important to be aware of a child's developmental level and mastery of certain skills and concepts involved in block play. Knowing this will help guide your expecta-

tions, while also noting when certain milestones are achieved. Also, over time, if you notice that a particular child's constructions haven't changed or become more complex, it may be that he or she may need encouragement with new accessories or ideas.

6. *How does a child interact with others?* Observe children's interactions to see how social issues such as sharing, cooperation, and taking turns are resolved. Note children's negotiating and problem-solving solutions. These observations will give you and parents valuable information about children's social development.

Use these observations to help gauge children's progress in specific areas. Reviewing your notes, you might find that a child rarely interacted with others and made only flat structures in September. But by March, the child was exchanging ideas with others and working on more complex buildings, indicating progress in developing creativity, motor control, problem-solving abilities, and self-confidence.

LEARNING AND

This chart illustrates the versatility of blocks and how block play can contribute to social, emotional, physical, and cognitive growth. Under each area, more specific skills and concepts are listed.

Each entry begins with a description of the skill or concept and how it is developed through block play. "Ways to assist" are suggestions you can use to promote further development. "Developmental considerations" are guidelines to help you know what to expect from younger children (age 2-3) and from older children (age 4-5). Naturally, behavior varies greatly at all ages, so these should be viewed as guidelines only.

PHOTO: MONKMEYER PRESS/ © GEORGE GOODWIN

GROWING WITH BLOCKS

SOCIAL/EMOTIONAL

COOPERATION AND SHARING

Block play offers many ways to help children develop these key social skills. They may build structures independently, then discover that by using these structures cooperatively, play is often more fun. They may also begin to see that cleanup is easier when many hands are helping.

Ways to assist:
- Help children learn the language of sharing: "I'm using the truck now. You can have it when I'm through." Acknowledge when they ask politely for materials.
- Help children solve disputes. "Let's talk about how you can both have what you want," is an irresistible invitation to both parties, because it implies a win-win resolution.
- Make suggestions for cooperative play, but never demand it: "Look at all these great buildings. It looks like a town. I wonder if the people in Jennifer's hotel would like to eat in Jason's restaurant?"

Developmental considerations:
- It is natural for younger children not to play cooperatively or to share easily. They start out in "solitary play," then develop patterns of "parallel play" where they will play near each other, doing the same thing.
- By ages four and five, children are usually ready to play cooperatively. They are then more likely to share ideas and interact with each other.

SELF-ESTEEM

Block building enhances self-esteem by offering opportunities for success. There is no "right" or "wrong" way to create a building, so there is less chance for a child to experience failure. The act of building and then knocking down a structure can help children feel powerful and in control.

Ways to encourage self-esteem:
- Show interest in children's constructions by observing in the block area and by inviting kids to talk about their work.
- Try not to tell children how to build something. Acknowledge their constructions by describing what you see: "Gee, Hadi, I see your bridge is so much longer than it was a minute ago!"
- Find ways to help children enjoy their successes by encouraging them to talk about their buildings, taking pictures of exceptional constructions, or telling parents about them.

Developmental considerations:
- Younger children enjoy the physical act of building up and crashing down their buildings. They feel powerful! As older children play, use nonjudgmental questions to find out why kids may be acting aggressively: "Gee, that monster must have been very angry to destroy this whole city. What made the monster so angry?"

DRAMATIC PLAY

Dramatic play in the block corner is different from make-believe play in the housekeeping center. Rather than "becoming" a character, a child manipulates objects to control a scene. Perhaps he or she will designate a character to symbolize herself or use blocks to symbolize food, a telephone, or other things. Nevertheless, the child is still using imagination, role-playing events she sees in daily life, or working through important emotional issues.

Ways to assist:
- Provide interesting accessories, including figures of small people, vehicles, animals, and furniture.
- Offer ideas and props to relate play to unit themes.

Developmental considerations:
- Younger children usually find the props more important than the blocks. They choose themes based on available accessories.
- At ages three and four, children often name their structures after they are built, which then determines the play themes.
- Children five and older tend to enter the block area with a theme in mind. A building is created as the setting for a drama that is acted out with props and sound effects.
- Older children also tend to work through emotional themes by staging scenes that re-enact events they have seen on television or experienced firsthand.

LEARNING AND

PHYSICAL

SENSORY PERCEPTION
Perception involves using the senses to gain information. Block play requires children to focus their eyes in a close visual space — good practice for reading. They must see an enclosure as having an inside and an outside space. They must measure a space with their eyes to select a block that spans it.

Ways to assist:
- Encourage children to use large blocks to make tunnels and bridges that they can fit into or under. To do this, children must visually determine the size of the open space and judge whether it's larger than their bodies.
- Talk about the texture of the blocks. Encourage children to describe how they feel — rough, smooth, soft, etc.
- Provide accessories that can fit inside of spaces. Then encourage children to give you a window on how they perceive: "How did you know that car would fit in your garage?"

Developmental considerations:
- Younger children often have a difficult time judging the size of their own bodies. They also have difficulty distinguishing foreground from background.
- Older children benefit from practice in distinguishing shapes on a background — a skill needed later on to make sense of a printed page.

FINE MOTOR
Block building requires eye-hand coordination. Children must control arm and hand movements to place one block on top of another and not bump the whole structure in the process. But the rewards are immediate when the structure emerges intact!

Ways to assist:
- Suggest — but don't push — that children test their fine-motor control by adding to their buildings: "Do you think you could make your skyscraper even taller?"
- Include accessories like ribbon or yarn that children might use to weave in and out of an arrangement of blocks.

Developmental considerations:
- It's more of a challenge for younger children to build without bumping. But they also exercise eye-hand coordination when they line up flat rows of blocks or lay them side by side.
- Practice at creating intricate buildings helps develop older children's motor development.

CREATIVE

CREATIVITY
Creativity involves combining things to make something new. That's one of the reasons blocks inspire such creativity. They are a familiar material that can be arranged and rearranged in endless ways.

Ways to assist:
- Change the accessories, even the blocks, from time to time. New materials spark new ideas.
- Suggest a challenge that encourages flexible thinking: "What are some ways we could make a roof for this building?"

Developmental considerations:
- Younger children tend to build without a final product in mind. When the creation starts to look like something, it gets a name.
- Older children usually set out to make something. They try new ideas, modifying them as needed.
- Ask children to explain their creations to help you appreciate their ideas. A preschooler may not have the motor skills to fully execute a brilliant idea.

GROWING WITH BLOCKS

COGNITIVE

AESTHETIC APPRECIATION

Children become aware of the pleasing effects of symmetry and balance as they create with blocks. A sense of confidence in their own artistic judgment may develop as they combine blocks in appealing ways.

Ways to assist:
■ Display prints of works by artists who use simple shapes and patterns that young children would find interesting. Help older children identify the patterns and shapes — they later may decide to incorporate them into their constructions.
■ Observe and comment on examples of balance and symmetry: "It looks like you have as many blocks on this side of your building as on the other side. Both sides look the same."
■ Provide art materials for children to use that would add color and detail to their structures.

Developmental considerations:
■ With younger children, aesthetic appreciation is often in the eye of the beholder. They tend to simply group blocks together until they find an arrangement they like. But the pride is genuine when they call for you to "look at what I made."
■ Older children are capable of creating symmetrical buildings and structures with involved and often striking patterns. They will appreciate leaving up a building every now and then so they can admire their handiwork!

LANGUAGE/PREREADING

During block play, children are learning vocabulary for concepts of form, size, location, and relationship: "This one is longer than that one." "Put it next to the triangle." "I need a tiny one to fit in here." Blocks encourage conversation between children and, in the process, they find new words to express their needs while learning new words from each other.

Ways to assist:
■ Invite children to brainstorm lists of words related to their buildings. What are the parts of a house? What do we need to make a block city?
■ Develop chants and songs to go along with block building.
■ Model language for children, either by using a puppet who can describe the buildings it sees or by playing near or with a child, talking as you build.

Developmental considerations:
■ Younger children absorb language by hearing others use it. Block play encourages language development in a meaningful setting, where being able to communicate can enhance play. Words that are first heard in the block corner are often more easily remembered.
■ Older children will enjoy seeing written labels on their buildings. Encourage them to make the labels, using invented spellings, to help them move from speaking to writing words.

PROBLEM-SOLVING

One of the most important skills kids can learn is the ability to recognize a problem, to think of solutions, and to try ideas until one works. Because block building presents an abundance of problems ("I don't have the block I need." "The roof won't stay up.") it offers children meaningful practice in problem-solving.

Ways to assist:
Teach children the steps to follow to solve a problem:
■ Identify the problem: "We have a problem here. Some people are building in front of the door, and that's not safe. How can we solve this problem?"
■ Think of as many different ways to solve a problem as you can: "Those are good ideas. What else could we try?"
■ Choose the best idea.
■ Try that idea first.
■ If it doesn't work, try another idea.
■ Keep trying until one works.

Developmental considerations:
■ Younger children are more likely to become frustrated with a problem and simply walk away or knock the building down. They need more support and help with ideas: "Don't give up. Maybe you can try this and see if it works."
■ Older children are more likely to ask for and to try different ideas. Encourage them to explain their solutions: "I saw that you were having trouble before. How did you solve the problem?"

LEARNING AND

COGNITIVE

SCIENCE CONCEPTS

Science experiences can develop children's observation, comparison, classification, and prediction skills. Children practice these key skills in the block area every day. In the process, they get exposure to other scientific principles, such as gravity and balance.

Ways to assist:
■ Encourage children to use the blocks to experiment. For example, help children build a ramp, then have them roll balls down it. Asking, "How could you change the ramp to make the ball go faster?" may lead to the discovery that objects move faster down a steeper incline.
■ Set up activities that require children to make predictions: "What do you think will happen if we put this block over here?"
■ Sharpen skills by asking children to describe what they see or to make comparisons: "Does Jamie's building look just like Kim's?"

Developmental considerations:
■ Younger children get a rudimentary introduction to balance as they erect block towers, and to gravity when the blocks fall. Exposure to these forces prepares them for later understanding, but discussion of these concepts is beyond them.
■ Older children, who are choosing blocks for particular reasons, are more able to engage in activities that ask them to observe, compare, and classify.

SHAPES

Block building encourages children to manipulate shapes and to discover their various properties. As children build with shapes, the concept that all things are made up of shapes is also reinforced.

Ways to assist:
■ Focus children's attention on the shapes they use: "Raul, is that a triangle block in your house? What other shapes did you use?"
■ Assign specific shapes to individual kids at cleanup time.
■ Challenge older children to build using only one kind of shape. As they try to make a stable building with triangles, for example, they begin to appreciate the qualities of different shapes.

Developmental considerations:
■ As younger children carry blocks around, they gain a sense of different shapes by feeling how sides and edges vary.
■ Older children learn the names and properties of shapes as they build in more involved ways.

PATTERNS

Much of learning later on involves recognizing and understanding patterns — in reading, math, science, and other subject areas as well. Block building offers children opportunities to create patterns and is a starting place for understanding the concept of a pattern as something that repeats itself.

Ways to assist:
■ Point out patterns that appear in children's constructions: "Emily, I see you've used a big block, then a little block, then a big block, then a little block to build your tower. What size block will you use next?"
■ Find a pattern in the room, such as a cinderblock wall, and challenge children to duplicate it using blocks: "Let me see if you can use the blocks to make a pretend wall on the floor that looks like this real wall."

Developmental considerations:
■ Because younger children don't build with an idea in mind, patterns they create are usually accidental. But once they see a pattern, they'll continue it.
■ Older children will choose blocks with a pattern in mind. As they become more adept builders, they create patterns of increasing complexity that appear in a vertical tower or a construction on the floor.

GROWING WITH BLOCKS

CLASSIFYING AND SORTING

Recognizing likenesses and differences is an important readiness skill. Block play offers numerous opportunities to classify objects by physical attributes, then to sort those that are alike into groups. You will see children do this quite naturally when they choose blocks that are all the same.

Ways to assist:
■ Organize the block storage area so that it's necessary for kids to sort the blocks as they put them away. (See "Planning for Play in the Block Area," pages 25-34, for a sample system.)
■ Encourage children to build structures that are the same in some way. This should not be a competition but a discovery experience as they see how their structures are alike and different.
■ At cleanup time, ask individuals to pick up all the blocks of one shape or size.

Developmental considerations:
■ Younger children may appear not to notice different shapes. Yet, they then may choose a favorite shape and build only with that one — indicating they have considered likenesses and differences in choosing the shape they like best.
■ Some older children are so fascinated with the process of classifying and sorting that cleanup becomes the highlight of their time in the block area!

ORDERING AND COMPARING

Understanding which of two objects is "bigger" or how to order a set of objects from shortest to longest are concepts that come more easily to kids when they have had experience with blocks. The process of block building quite naturally involves comparing blocks for size and shape, and ordering blocks in a construction from biggest on the bottom to smallest on top.

Ways to assist:
■ Talk about the different sizes of constructions with children: "Let's see whose building is taller. Melanie's garage or Arthur's hotel? What do you think?"
■ Occasionally, help children use string to measure several constructions, labeling each string with a child's name. Then tack the strings on a wall in order from shortest to tallest.
■ Listen for conversations that demonstrate children are comparing objects. "I need a bigger block." "Here, try this one, it's bigger than yours." Comment to reinforce the concepts and the sharing: "You're looking carefully, Aaron. That bigger block is just what Michael needs."

Developmental considerations:
■ Younger children often first demonstrate a sense of ordering by arranging blocks by length.
■ Older children are more able to respond to requests like "find a block that is longer."

COUNTING AND NUMBER CONCEPTS

Having concrete manipulatives like blocks to hold and to set aside as they count reinforces one-to-one correspondence for children. As well, the meaning of numbers — that ten blocks is a bigger armful to carry than five blocks — is more apparent when kids can see and feel the amounts for themselves.

Ways to assist:
■ Reinforce the concept that a number represents a set of objects by asking children to count the blocks in a building, then labeling it with that number.
■ At cleanup time, count blocks with older children to compare the numbers: "Let's count these blocks together. There should be four arches and six pillars." After counting each group and placing them on the shelves, you can ask children: "Which group has more blocks, the arches or the pillars?"

Developmental considerations:
■ When younger children "count," they are often parroting words. Nevertheless, counting with children and talking about "how many" sets the groundwork for developing number concepts.
■ When older children work with real objects, they can begin to understand that a number represents a set of objects.

USING BLOCKS WITH CHILDREN WHO HAVE SPECIAL NEEDS

Block play is a valuable learning experience for all children. Therefore, playing with blocks can help children with special needs acquire the same important skills and concepts as other children. It also offers both special-needs children and nondisabled children opportunities to play and enjoy blocks together. By adapting your environment, then observing and facilitating children's natural interactions with one another, you can make block play accessible to and enjoyable for every child.

HELPING SPECIAL CHILDREN MAKE THE MOST OF BLOCK PLAY

Many of the "rules" for introducing special-needs children to blocks are the same as those for nondisabled kids. However, these children may, from time to time, need more guidance and structure. You'll want to introduce blocks gradually, giving children time to explore and play freely. If a child loses interest quickly, model or suggest ways to extend play: "I wonder where else we can make our road go."

Once children are familiar with the materials, encourage them to build more independently: "We started the road, but can you make it longer?"

Help children with special needs to interact successfully with others by teaching them how to share and how to follow the rules of the block area. Encourage interaction by drawing a child's attention to others playing near-by: "Robin is using little blocks." Or, show a child what others are doing in the block area: "Jason is making a bridge. Would you like to build something, too?"

You may also need to help a child with special needs respond to the overtures of others. Children with special needs often fail to acknowledge peers who approach them. When this happens consistently, the other children may give up trying to be friendly. Show or tell a child what to do: "Mario wants to join us. Is that OK?"

Because each child with a disability has unique needs, it's important to work with parents and therapists to gain

PHOTO: SUSAN RICHMAN

insights and techniques for working with individual children. However, there are general patterns of behavior and needs associated with different disabilities. The following should help in gauging what to expect and in understanding how to help children with specific impairments.

WORKING WITH CHILDREN WITH SPECIAL PHYSICAL CONDITIONS

Visually Impaired Children

Because children with limited sight are also limited in their ability to freely explore their environment, they are often delayed in motor skills. They may also have difficulty with size and spatial relationships. Block play offers opportunities to develop these skills and concepts. Here are some guidelines to keep in mind.

You can:

■ Gradually increase the number of blocks offered. Children with visual limitations may not be as experienced with blocks. Give them a small number

of shapes to start. As they become more comfortable with blocks, increase the number and variety.

■ Encourage independence. Help visually impaired kids function as independently as possible by enabling them to take part in all aspects of block play — including cleanup. Trace each block shape on cardboard, cut it out, and tape it to the corresponding shelf. Children can then trace the shapes with their fingers to find blocks and to know where they belong.

Provide a small wagon for a child to transport chosen blocks and to keep them close at hand.

Hearing-Impaired Children

These children are often delayed in language, readiness skills, and social development. The amount of delay generally correlates to the degree of hearing loss. Block play offers important opportunities to develop cognitive and social skills in a meaningful context.

You can:

■ Be observant and supportive. While hearing-impaired kids won't require special physical arrangements, they need lots of help with language and social interaction. Assist by making sure they understand the rules of the block area. Act out the rules and post pictures as reminders. Teach children the language that will help them be accepted by others such as, "May I play?" and, "It's my/your turn."

■ Facilitate communication. You'll also need to work with nondisabled children to encourage these interactions. Suggest that children use simple language and look directly at the hearing-impaired peer when talking.

Orthopedically Impaired Children

Children with orthopedic impairments will benefit from block play in practicing a variety of motor skills: using both hands at the same time in different ways; using one hand to assist the other; transferring objects from one

FACILITATING CHILDREN'S INTERACTIONS

To develop a spirit of acceptance in your room, it's important to encourage all children to respect each other as peers. When you observe interactions between disabled children and nondisabled children, watch to see if they need help to communicate with each other. If so, be very matter of fact and understanding so that the disabled child does not feel singled out or embarrassed. Here are some suggestions that can be helpful with older preschoolers when there seems to be a situation when your intervention would help facilitate their interaction.

■ With hearing-impaired children: Suggest that "hearing" children gently touch the hearing-impaired child on the arm to get his or her attention, especially if this child doesn't respond right away. Encourage hearing children to use simple

language and gestures when communicating, and look directly into the hearing-impaired child's eyes when speaking. This will be helpful for hearing-impaired children who read lips.
■ With mentally retarded children: Encourage children to use simple language and gestures when communicating.
■ With visually impaired children: Children can describe their constructions to visually impaired peers, and allow them to touch or look closely at their block structures.
■ With orthopedically impaired children: As they play together, observe to see if nondisabled children take over and do things for these children. Nondisabled children may be tempted to build a construction for a disabled child, for fear of their (or the child's) construction falling over. Help them understand how much fun it is for the child to create his or her own structure — just like it is for them.

hand to the other; opening and closing fingers and grasping, holding, and releasing objects; and enhancing eye-hand coordination.

You can:
■ Seek ways to help children join others. Whenever possible, let these children play with others on the floor. The best position for most orthopedically impaired kids is on the tummy with a bolster under the chest. This helps to raise the upper body and leaves the arms free to build. A child might also sit in a corner, using the two walls for support, or sit on a chair with the legs cut off. Use a belt to secure the child to the chair in an upright position.

If a child cannot leave a wheelchair, place a large tray across the arms of the chair. Encourage others to join the child in building on the tray.

■ Encourage horizontal building. A child with involuntary movements or abnormal startle reflexes may knock over stacked blocks and become discouraged, so encourage horizontal building. (This is also recommended for visually impaired children.) For a change of pace, occasionally assist the child in a stacking activity or suggest the child stack two or three blocks to begin a tower that others can complete.

CHILDREN WITH SPECIAL MENTAL AND EMOTIONAL CONDITIONS

Mentally Retarded Children
These children function at lower levels of cognitive and social development and may display difficult behaviors, such as aggression or withdrawal. They need lots of time to learn and to practice skills.

You can:
■ Introduce blocks gradually. When you first introduce mentally retarded children to the block area, give each about five blocks of the same shape and size. When kids are comfortable with these, increase the number and variety.

■ Offer lots of encouragement. These children need a lot of motivation to try new tasks, even when they have successfully mastered others. So begin by modeling a task: "Look, Kyle, I put a block on this block. Now you try it. You did it! Can you add another one?" Talk about the task and what the child is doing, and encourage the child to talk, too.

■ Help children prepare for transitions in advance. Mentally retarded children often have trouble coping with change. About five minutes before cleanup, announce that it's almost time to put the blocks away. Then repeat the reminder several more times. You can give the child a cleanup job, such as putting away two blocks.

Emotionally Impaired Children
For children who have been professionally diagnosed as emotionally impaired or emotionally disturbed, block play can help them gain self-confidence, learn to stay on task, and provide opportunities for social interactions. Try to insure that these children attempt tasks at their own ability levels and be supportive of their efforts.

You can:
■ Review rules. When children's emotional problems result in aggressiveness, the block area can become the scene of fights over materials and space. Try to avoid these problems by frequently reviewing the rules for appropriate behavior and by assigning blocks to each child. Monitor aggressive behavior, and acknowledge a child when he or she plays amicably with others.

■ Acknowledge interactions. For children who tend to be withdrawn, use block play to encourage interaction with peers through parallel play. Position the child near others. Watch for any natural interactions that may occur, and encourage them if both children seem interested. "Maybe Jane can park her car in your new parking lot, Andrea."

TALKING TO PARENTS
ABOUT BLOCK PLAY

Whether block play, dramatic play, water play, or other play activities, it's important to communicate the developmental benefits of these play experiences to parents. Although there often isn't anything tangible to show at the end of the day, there may be many valuable insights and observations to share.

Parent conferences and meetings, or pickup and drop-off times, are opportunities to discuss the value of children's play experiences. Here are some ideas that may help convey to parents the importance and value of playing with blocks.

BE SPECIFIC

The more concrete and specific you can be with parents regarding their child's experience with blocks, the better. Observing children during block play and noting what takes place will help you be more informative with parents. You can describe a child's constructions while relaying to parents exactly what the child was saying while playing. Then follow this up with any new skills or discoveries the child experienced. For example:

"Today (or yesterday) Joya built a large palace that had many rooms and stairways. Together we counted all the rooms and stairs. Then she added dragons, horses, and families to the scene and developed a story around them. Building such a large palace with so many rooms showed tremendous growth in her fine-motor development. Her interest in counting the rooms gave us some added practice with math. The drama she developed was complex and demonstrated how creative and imaginative her thinking has become."

Explaining block play to parents this way helps them appreciate and under-stand their child's experience with blocks.

SHOW EXAMPLES

One of the best ways to help parents appreciate their children's work in the block area is to show it to them. Although it won't always be possible, leave up a construction from time to time. Or take an instant picture of a great structure and let the child take the momento home. The child's description of his or her structure could also accompany the photo. Pictures could also be kept in a scrapbook or displayed in the block corner for children and parents to enjoy together.

GET PARENTS INVOLVED

You can also help parents appreciate the fun and skill that goes into block building by letting them get down on the floor and play! Hold an evening workshop and devote 30 minutes to working with blocks.

As they build, ask parents to think about the thought processes and physical skills they are using.

Encourage them to think about the kinds of social skills that are required to share materials and space. As they create, ask questions or take dictation as they describe their structures. All the while, explain that these are the kinds of activities you would be doing with children to make the most of their block play.

USE THIS GUIDE AS A RESOURCE

Many sections of this guide can help you communicate the value of block play to parents. Photocopy the following pages and send them home:

■ The parent letter, "Helping Your Child Get the Most From Blocks," page 24.

■ The chart, "Learning and Growing With Blocks," pages 14-19.

■ "Blocks and More Blocks," pages 30-31.

■ "Accessories That Stimulate Creative Play," pages 32-33.

■ Activity Pages, pages 38-77. Send home an activity along with the parent letter on the following page. Then send home a new one each week. Or you can leave them on a table, or put them in a "pocket" on a bulletin board for parents.

LEARNING THROUGH BLOCK PLAY
A MESSAGE TO PARENTS

Dear Parent,

Block play can be an exciting, inspiring, and greatly satisfying experience for your child. You can extend the benefits of block play at home. By observing and assisting your child during play, you can help your child get more learning and enjoyment from playing with blocks. Here are some suggestions:

Block Play at Home

1. Try to create a space for block play. It's best to store blocks on a low shelf rather than in a toy box. Your child will then be able to see the blocks that he or she wants to play with, and the blocks are less likely to be damaged. Try to find an area in your house or apartment where your child can spread out — at least for a while.

2. Follow your child's lead during play. Try to think of yourself as an assistant to your child — allowing her to create the drama and direct the play. You can ask questions that enhance your child's play and clarify the drama as it unfolds. "That castle just tumbled down. What happened to it?" If your child requests your participation you can say, "OK. How can I help? What would you like me to do?" Your child will enjoy block play more if you show an interest in what he or she is doing.

3. Encourage your child to describe the constructions he or she is making. If your child seems interested, this is a good way for her to verbalize what is happening and elaborate on what is being created. Rather than saying "That's nice. What is it?" You might start a conversation by saying, "Gee, this is getting bigger and bigger. You have used so many little blocks, too. Can you tell me about it?" This way you're describing what you see, and are not assuming that it is something in particular. Often children create without a final product in mind. Leave the question open enough for your child to describe what she is making.

4. Help your child find ways to solve problems. Naturally, it's tempting to add the roof yourself when you can see your child has tried many times and failed. But your child will feel more confident and successful when she figures out the solutions independently. Try these steps to help your child be a better problem-solver:

- Find out what she has tried already, then encourage your child to think of some more solutions. This is where you might offer an idea or two.
- Encourage your child to try the new ideas until one works. Offer praise when the problem is solved!
- Ask your child to describe the problem. She has to know what it is in order to solve it.

MAKE YOUR OWN BLOCKS!

While wooden unit blocks and small table blocks can be found in toy stores, you can also make your own blocks. Let your child help you make blocks out of boxes.

- Stuff different-size boxes, such as empty diaper boxes and clean cardboard milk cartons, with crumpled newspaper.

- Tape boxes securely, then cover them with colorful self-stick paper.

- Your child will enjoy using these blocks to build large structures.

PLANNING FOR PLAY
IN THE BLOCK AREA

- **KEEPING THE BLOCK AREA EXCITING AND MANAGEABLE**
- **ACCESSORIES THAT STIMULATE CREATIVE PLAY**

PHOTO: DIANA KASSIR

KEEPING THE BLOCK AREA
EXCITING and MANAGEABLE

The care you take to set up the block area communicates its importance to children. While planning, consider not only where it works best in the classroom, but how its arrangement can inspire creative and cooperative play among your children. You can begin by evaluating the area from a developmental point of view — how this area can best meet the needs of your twos, threes, fours, or fives.

Making the area "work" involves finding ways to organize materials so that kids can play and clean up with a minimum of teacher direction. It also involves providing the right types of blocks and the right mix of accessories to encourage the kind of play that helps to develop skills and concepts.

This section will offer ways to keep the area exciting, fresh, and manageable for your children. Included are suggestions for finding a location and for furnishing the area; tips on organizing materials and facilitating cleanup; and information on developmental considerations, blocks to stock, and accessories to provide.

LOCATE A SPACE FOR ACTIVE PLAY

Where should you begin? First, take a look around your room to find an area that is spacious enough for children to spread out and play comfortably. Keep in mind that areas away from doors, sinks, or cubbies, where block constructions cannot be knocked over by accident, are best. The area itself can become a safety hazard if play extends into these high traffic areas.

With that in mind, what are some good locations to consider? Most block areas function best when they are placed next to other active areas in your room. The housekeeping area, for example, is a "high energy" area and the materials and props in this area combine nicely with blocks. Quieter areas such as art, reading, science, and others can be problematic because children in these areas could be disturbed by the sounds and activity in the block area.

If possible, try to reserve the area you select for block play only, instead of having it double for circle time and other activities. In this way, you can offer children the option of leaving some constructions intact for a day or two — a difficult task when the area plays double duty.

CONSIDER YOUR CHILDREN'S NEEDS

As with other areas, the block area best suits your children when its physical setup is designed to complement their developmental level. A good rule of thumb for all ages is to start the year with less, not more. Fewer blocks and accessories are less likely to overwhelm children with choices or a time-consuming cleanup. As you observe children at play, decide when to add more. For example, when children seem less drawn to the area or when their building becomes repetitive, add some new materials. Consider the following guidelines, but remember that stages rather than ages should determine your approach.

■ **Twos** – A block corner specifically designed for twos might include a set of large cardboard blocks and three or four wooden vehicles to push along "roads."

Just a few unit blocks are adequate for this age. Every few weeks, add some blocks of another shape or a few new accessories.

Threes and Fours – A block corner for three- and four-year-olds will need more space for building and more blocks of different shapes, as well as simple accessories — vehicles, people, and animals. Keep in mind that there must be enough interesting materials to entice children to the area and a sufficient number of blocks for kids to play together.

Fives – Almost from the beginning of the year, fives are ready for a fairly sophisticated assortment of blocks and accessories. Because they will want to build elaborate structures and use the creations as the settings for dramatic play, give them plenty of space and have plenty of interesting materials on hand to fuel their imaginations.

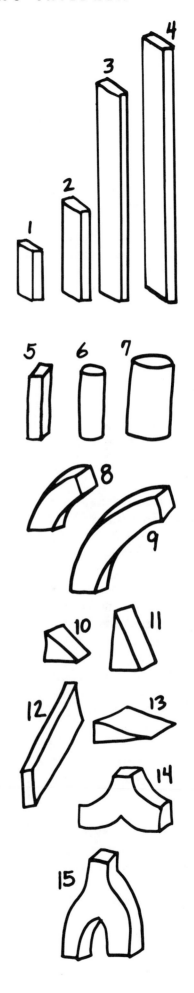

HOW MANY BLOCKS ARE ENOUGH?

The following chart has been adapted from *Play Equipment for the Nursery School* by Jessie Stanton and Alma Weisberg (Bank Street). Keep in mind that these are guidelines for 7-10 children and make adjustments for your group.

Block Recommendations for Three- to Five-Year-Olds
(for 7-10 children)

Block Type	3 years	4 years	5 years
(1) Half units	24	24	30
(2) Units	54	96	110
(3) Double units	48	70	95
(4) Quadruple units	24	24	36
(5) Pillars	12	24	36
(6) Small cylinders	10	16	20
(7) Large cylinders	10	12	16
(8) Circular curves	6	8	10
(9) Elliptical curves	4	8	10
(10) Pairs of small triangles	4	8	9
(11) Pairs of large triangles	4	8	12
(12) Floor boards — 11"	6	15	30
(13) Ramps	6	16	20
(14) Right-angle switches	0	4	8
(15) Y switches	2	2	4
Blocks not illustrated			
Roofboards	0	6	10
X-switches	0	4	8
Half pillars	0	6	8
Total	214	351	472

(Numbers in parentheses refer to drawing)

From *Play Equipment for the Nursery School* by Jessie Stanton, Alma Weisberg, and the faculty of the Bank Street School for Children.

While the ideal would be to have enough space and blocks for any number of children to play with in the block area at one time, the reality is that you will probably need to set a limit to avoid overcrowding. A simple means of identifying whose turn it is to play with blocks usually works well with older threes, and with fours and fives. Here's an idea:

1. Make a pocket chart with spaces for the number of children who may play in your block area at once.
2. Hang the chart near the entrance to your block area.
3. Provide laminated name tags for each child to place in a free pocket before playing in the center.

This system encourages decision-making as children are asked to make a choice by placing their name on the chart. Independence is fostered as children can determine for themselves whether or not there is "room for one more."

While this system works well for older preschoolers, the block area for twos and young threes will probably require an adult to determine how many can play comfortably.

KEEP IT SIMPLE AND SAFE

Knowing what is needed, and what is not needed, when furnishing your children's block area can make all the difference in how children play and interact while building. Here are some guidelines to keep in mind:

■ *Keep the area spacious.* To give children as much building space as possible, simpler is better when choosing furnishings for the block corner. Avoid having unnecessary tables or other furniture pieces in the area.

■ *Use low shelves for storage.* Two or more large, low shelves are really all you need for storing blocks and acces-

sories. Hinged shelf units make good storage areas because they are very stable and can be closed when you don't want children playing with blocks.

■ *Use shelves to separate the area.* Mark off the area with shelves or other dividers positioned so that they face the wall and provide a boundary for the block area. (To make sure the shelves are stable, back each with another shelf or with a table.) While you want to give children plenty of space, block play can easily expand into main traffic areas of the room if you do not establish boundaries. This will eliminate the risk of children tripping or buildings being knocked over

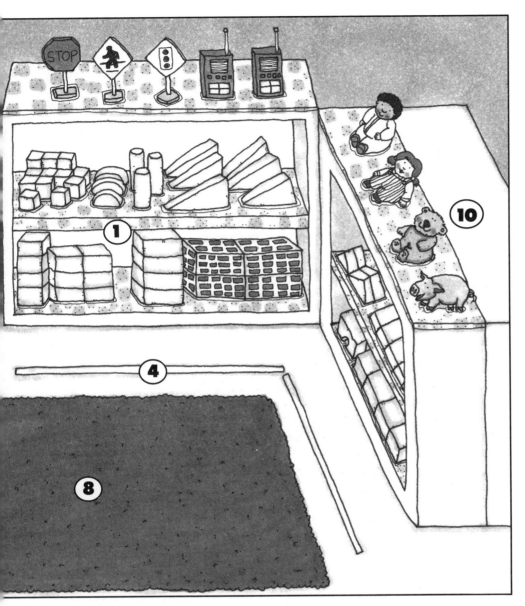

AN IDEAL SET-UP

The illustration at left shows some simple and safe ways to set up your block area. The numbers in the illustration coincide with the suggestions below. Please refer to "Keep It Simple and Safe," pages 28-30, for more detailed guidelines about the suggestions that follow.

1. Develop a storage arrangement with matching "puzzle bases" for easy cleanup.

2. Display larger accessories on shelves with matching outlines for easy access and to facilitate cleanup.

3. Display smaller accessories in clear plastic boxes, labeled with simple outlines, for easy identification.

4. Use colored plastic tape to mark off building boundaries.

5. Mark off "parking areas" for large vehicles with colored tape.

6. Display posters and photographs of city scenes to inspire children's play and constructions.

7. Hang a bulletin board at children's eye level to display their drawings, dictated stories, and photographs of their work.

8. Use low-pile carpet to muffle the sound of falling blocks.

9. Provide a sign-up system to play in the area.

10. Back storage shelves with other shelf units for added stability.

by passing children or adults.

■ *Cover the area with low-pile carpet.* Provide some low-pile indoor/outdoor carpet for children to sit and build on. (Low-pile carpet is best — raised patterns or shag can make block constructions uneven.)

Carpet will prevent children from sitting on a cold floor, and will also muffle the sound of falling blocks, making them less noisy. This way children building in the block area can enjoy the sound of falling blocks without disturbing children in other areas of the room.

■ *Set building boundaries.* To enable children to get to the shelves without disturbing other builders, put a line of colored plastic tape on the floor about 12 inches from the shelves, parallel to them. Then direct children not to build between the line and the shelves.

■ *Inspire play with pictures.* Display pictures of different types of buildings, homes, vehicles, highways, and bridges for inspiration. Pictures of men, women, and children of different races and physical abilities doing a variety of jobs communicates that the block area is for everyone. Try to include photographs of buildings and people who work in your neighborhood or town. They can reflect the cultural/ethnic diversity and architecture of your community.

■ *Display children's work.* Add a low display area on one wall for displaying

MAKE YOUR OWN BIG BLOCKS

You'll find these homemade blocks are simple to make, only requiring everyday materials. Ask parents to donate diaper boxes and cartons to help your collection grow.

DIAPER-BOX BLOCKS

What you need: empty diaper boxes, newspaper, masking tape, scissors, and self-stick paper (optional).

What you do: Stuff the empty diaper boxes with crumpled newspaper, then tape securely. Cover with decorative self-stick paper for visual appeal.

MILK-CARTON BLOCKS

What you need: clean cardboard milk or juice cartons in half-pint, pint, quart, or half-gallon sizes (two of a size are needed for each block), scissors, newspaper, masking tape, and self-stick paper (optional).

What you do: Cut off the triangular tops from the cartons. Take two same-size cartons. Crumple newspaper and stuff one carton, packing tightly. Then put the open end of the stuffed carton into the open end of the empty carton, and slide together as far as they will go. Tape securely. If desired, cover with decorative self-stick paper.

PAPER-BAG BLOCKS

What you need: paper grocery sacks, newspaper, masking tape, and non-toxic markers.

What you do: You can ask the children to use the markers to decorate the grocery sacks before you make them into blocks. Then stuff the sacks with crumpled newspaper until full. Push the paper down a bit so you can fold over the top, and tape securely.

block-related drawings and dictated stories. If you take photographs of your children with their buildings, they could also be posted here or arranged in an inexpensive plexiglass frame. It's a wonderful self-esteem booster for your children.

Organize Blocks and Accessories

When blocks are stored on shelves, rather than in a box or bin, it's easier for kids to select the blocks they need and to sort blocks by shape as they put them away. This not only helps you stay organized, but it also gives children a sense of control. They can find what they want and know where things go.

The storage suggestions that follow will help foster independence during block play and cleanup:

■ *Develop a storage arrangement that's easy for children to follow.* Store blocks in a top-down/left-right/small-large pattern. It helps children practice sequencing, seriation, and visual-discrimination skills. Here's how to do it:
1. Put the smallest blocks in the upper left-hand corner of the shelf.
2. Place the next largest blocks to their right, and continue until the top shelf fills up.
3. Then start on the left of the shelf below and continue the progression.
4. Eventually the heaviest blocks will be on the bottom shelves, adding stability. Be sure to place rectangles sideways, so children can see their lengths.
■ *Create puzzle bases to facilitate cleanup.* Once you arrive at a storage arrangement you like, consider "puzzle" bases for the blocks on each shelf. This will enable your children to put blocks away by matching their shapes to the outlines. Here's how:
1. Cut a piece of butcher paper to fit the length and width of each shelf.
2. Arrange the first layer of blocks on the paper, and trace around each one with a marking pen.
3. Remove the paper and cover it with clear self-stick paper. Then secure it to the shelf with tape or tacks. Do this for each shelf.

This system creates an orderly arrangement and can easily be changed when necessary. Children cover the outlines while putting blocks away, forming the first layer of blocks. Then they can put other blocks of the same shape on top of these, building vertically.

■ *Store and display block accessories for easy access.* Try storing larger accessories on the top or inside of shelves to attract interest. Give these their own silhouettes on paper to mark their spots.
1. Also try using clear plastic storage boxes. They allow children to see what's inside and work well for holding many types of small figures. Designate a particular spot on a shelf for each box of accessories by labeling each outline with a picture of the contents cut from old catalogs or toy boxes.
2. Mark off "parking areas" on the floor in the block area with plastic tape (masking tape leaves a sticky residue) for large vehicles.

■ *Use space savers to conserve room.* For programs with limited space, such as some family day-care programs, try folding shelves on casters, which you can close and roll away to store blocks and accessories. Sturdy plastic crates, placed on their sides so that they are open like a shelf, could also be used.

BLOCKS AND MORE BLOCKS

When we hear the word blocks, we may tend to think of wooden unit blocks, but today there are so many others to choose from. Large hollow wooden, plastic, or cardboard blocks; large foam-rubber blocks covered with vinyl; and/or small wooden table blocks can supplement your unit blocks. They are fun for children to play with and offer unique ways to promote their physical development and learning.

Most blocks are expensive, but remember that you get a lot of learning value for your money. Good quality hardwood blocks will last for the life of your program. The more blocks and interesting accessories there are, the greater learning potential they will hold while enriching children's play. With a wide variety of shapes to choose from, buildings and constructions become more complex and exciting.

A Guide to Different Blocks

With so many materials and sizes to choose from, selecting blocks for the block area can be quite a task. Use this list to help remind you of the options available when purchasing blocks.

Unit Blocks – These were first developed in 1914 by Carolyn Pratt, a progressive early childhood educator who founded The City and Country School in New York City. Wooden unit blocks come in a wide variety of shapes — rectangles, squares, triangles, cylinders, half circles, quarter circles, arches, "switches," and more.

The single-unit rectangle is the "starting block." It is 1 3/8 inches by 2 3/4 inches by 5 1/2 inches. All other blocks relate to the size of the single unit so that two single units equal one double unit; two double units make one quadruple unit; a triangle equals the length of a single unit cut diagonally; and a pillar is as tall as the length of a single unit. These relationships help to encourage mathematical discoveries as kids play.

Large Hollow Wooden Blocks – Made of hardwood, these blocks come in squares, rectangles, and triangular ramps. Although they take up a good deal of space, they are an excellent addition to both indoor and outdoor play for fours and older. Children can use them to make houses, vehicles, and other structures which they can actually use in dramatic play.

It's easiest to store large hollow blocks on the floor. Use tape lines to outline where specific blocks should go, placing the larger blocks on the floor and stacking smaller blocks on top. If you keep the blocks outside for playground use, you'll need a dry place to store them.

Large Hollow Plastic Blocks – There are several types of large plastic blocks. Most come in bright primary colors, and some will interlock. Kids can use them to make large, sturdy structures to get inside or to sit on top of. Like the hollow wooden blocks, they need to be used in a large open space. But they are light enough to be stored on open shelves or can be stacked on the floor.

Cardboard Blocks – Blocks made of reinforced cardboard are great to use with younger preschool children, though older children enjoy them, too. Measuring about one foot in length, they are light and allow the children the satisfaction of making something big. Cardboard blocks are fairly durable, but they are not recommended for playground use as moisture may ruin them.

Vinyl-Covered Foam Blocks – These large, easy-to-clean blocks are ideal for toddler programs. They are light enough for kids to lift and stack into high towers. Yet, because they are soft, they don't make a lot of noise or endanger anyone when they fall. Their bright colors warm up a room and they can be used in many different ways.

Table Blocks – As the name implies, these small versions of unit blocks are designed to be used on a table or on the floor. Some are natural wood, others are painted bright colors. Children often like to combine them with unit blocks to add finishing touches. You may also find ways to use them for teaching colors and for sorting activities.

Counting Cubes – These brightly colored one-inch wooden cubes are also used as accessories to the unit blocks. Children often decorate their buildings with them. They are fairly inexpensive and make a good addition to a set of unit blocks.

Parquetry Blocks – These small wooden blocks come in a variety of shapes, including diamonds and triangles. They are brightly colored and are fun to use to create repeating patterns or to decorate block buildings.

ACCESSORIES FOR BIG-BLOCK PLAY

Here's a starter list of materials that will make play with big blocks even more exciting. Ask kids for their ideas, too!

- carpet squares
- cardboard cylinders
- fabric pieces
- hard hats
- large traffic signs
- large vehicle toys
- license plates
- play dishes
- large sheets of acrylic plastic
- riding toys
- sheets and blankets
- steering wheels

ACCESSORIES
THAT STIMULATE CREATIVE PLAY

Accessories give children ideas for imaginative play and can extend block building to involve other themes. Changing accessories from time to time helps renew interest in blocks and stimulates new learning. Very young children are still finding out about what they can do with blocks, so accessories for twos and young threes should be the more familiar figures — vehicles, animals, people, and dollhouse furniture.

For all ages, it's wise to have two or more identical samples of popular accessories, such as cars and trucks. This not only reduces conflicts among older children but reinforces the emerging parallel play of twos, who like to sit near each other doing the same activity.

There is a wide variety of possible accessories for the block center. These include purchased materials as well as "found" items. But remember that too many accessories overwhelm children. They may start to hoard them or to focus on the properties of the accessories rather than on using them to accent their buildings.

Basic accessories, such as vehicles, dolls, and animals, should be available to children all the time. However, if you observe that children's play themes could potentially be enhanced with special accessories, introduce and allow your children to use them in their own way. For instance, "Here are some cotton and aluminum foil. You may be able to use them for something in your space station."

Accessories can also inspire new themes and creative ideas in the block area. Take time to discuss them during circle time by saying, "Here are some

MAKE YOUR OWN:
CULTURALLY DIVERSE STAND-UP PEOPLE & FAMILIES

If your program can't afford new dolls at this time, or if you want to add a family or two to your collection, here's a way to create your own:

■ **What you need:** Magazine pictures or photos of people of different races and ethnic groups. (For added fun, you can even use photos of your children.); cardboard; clear self-stick paper; plaster of Paris; and aerosol-can tops.

■ **What you do:** Cut out the pictures and mount them on cardboard. Laminate or cover each with clear self-stick paper. Then mix plaster of Paris and pour it into each aerosol-can top. Sink each figure into the plaster and let dry.

PHOTO: © ERIKA STONE 1990

bottle caps, and tiles I brought from home. Do you think you can use them in the block area? What could you do with them?" Later, leave them in the block area for children to use during play.

When selecting accessories, naturally screen for items that would be unsafe for children who continually put things in their mouths. Anything with sharp edges or that is smaller than the child's fist should be kept out of reach.

Here are some to think about:

Vehicles Look for small wooden and plastic cars, trucks, airplanes, buses, vans, boats, miniature road signs, and gas stations. The presence of vehicles may inspire kids to make roads, bridges, tunnels, or space stations! Road signs, billboards, and street signs can enhance play.

People Look for multiethnic wooden stand-up characters and flexible rubber people that represent family members and different occupations. Kids can use them to act out dramatic-play scenes involving families or community helpers.

Dollhouse Accessories Shop for flexible, multiethnic plastic dollhouse families and for sturdy dollhouse furniture. The presence of furniture and dolls inspires children to create houses, rooms, and castles. The dolls are also useful for acting out family routines or themes.

Animals Focus on wooden and plastic farm, forest, jungle, and underwater animals, as well as dinosaurs and dragons. Children's constructions and play will be far more imaginative and whimsical when a variety of real and make-believe animals are offered.

Towns Look for miniature towns with buildings, trees, people, and animals. These sets inspire children to arrange their own villages and make-believe lands. Concepts of space and relative size are reinforced.

Trains Shop for wooden railroad trains and tracks. Train sets are very popular. They can arrange the tracks and assemble the cars in different ways, and in the process, sequencing skills are reinforced.

"Found" Accessories To Enhance Play

Many discarded items can be used as accessories that add fun to building. As children are presented with interesting items to include in their play, they are encouraged to use creative thinking and problem-solving as they decide where to place them, how many to use, what they represent (if anything), and how everyday items are used to enhance a theme or drama.

Here are some to look for, but keep in mind that your children will discover some original "toss-aways" too, especially if you encourage them to bring some from home. While we have suggested uses for the ones below, allow your children to find their own ways to use them.

■ Aluminum foil can be wrapped around blocks to make silver skyscrapers, or used to make roofs or "swimming pools."

■ Blankets make wonderful caves, especially when using large blocks.

■ Bottle caps can decorate constructions, add to patterns, or become "faces" in enclosures.

■ Boxes can become rooms, trucks, barns, and bases for buildings.

■ Cardboard pieces can become the walls between apartments or roofs, while carpet squares and tiles make wonderful floors.

■ Coffee can lids and jar lids can decorate buildings or make headlights for vehicles.

■ Cotton can be fluffy snow, or bedding for dolls or animals.

■ Empty thread spools can decorate castles, as can colorful aerosol-can tops.

Do Your Accessories Create a Bias-Free Environment?

Stand-up dolls and other accessories for block play offer children a wonderful opportunity to develop play themes around people of different races and careers.

As children play with dolls that reflect the differences in their own families, racial or ethnic backgrounds, or lifestyles, they begin to learn about each other and appreciate the differences in themselves and others. Here are some questions to ask yourself as you select and collect accessories:

■ Do I have any accessories that promote negative stereotypes (such as cowboy and Indian sets)?

■ Are the dolls representative of different racial and ethnic groups — especially those of my class?

■ How do the dolls look? Are their features natural and lifelike?

■ Do the male and female "career dolls" represent nonsexist roles?

■ Is there an ample supply of "stand-up families," so that children can create many different family configurations, roles, and dramas?

■ Do the accessories appeal to both boys and girls?

■ What "found" materials can children bring from home that are interesting and different?

■ Are there "found" materials or accessories (such as miniature buildings) that reflect your particular community?

Rules to Build By

For children's safety as well as enjoyment, it's important to establish rules for block play. If possible, try to involve children in setting these rules. Write them on chart paper with diagrams, and post them in your block area. Some possible rules might include:

■ Blocks are for building, *not* for throwing.

■ Only four (or whatever number you decide works best) people in the block corner at one time.

■ Never take blocks from someone else's building without permission.

■ You may knock down your own building but not someone else's.

■ Take turns with friends when using blocks and toys.

■ Help clean up.

Be active in reminding children of the rules. Review them occasionally during safe times, such as circle time, when no one is on the spot for violating a rule. Encourage children to articulate the importance of certain rules by asking, "Why do you suppose this rule is important to remember?"

■ Film canisters can become castle turrets and towers.

■ Flashlights may encourage children to build enclosed structures with dark inner spaces to illuminate.

■ Modeling paste (such as Plasticine) can keep ice pop sticks upright for making trees or fences. Kids can shape clay into pretend food.

■ Old headphones inspire dramatic play around the roles of pilot, air traffic controller, or astronaut. An old radio or walkie-talkie may encourage detective dramas.

■ Paper-towel tubes may become telescopes, pillars, tunnels, or musical horns.

■ Pinecones can become pine trees in a small town. Shells can decorate and make patterns.

■ Plastic tubing can provide an attendant with a gas-pump hose, or an astronaut with a lifeline.

■ "Pretend" grass makes good "hay."

■ Small ceramic tiles can form patterns and walkways, and enclose boundaries.

■ Stones can become designs or make enclosures. They're especially fun to use outside with sand.

■ Yarn can connect spaces, create shapes, and "fence off" areas.

QUICK TIPS FOR CLEANUP

Cleanup time can be stressful for both you and your children. The key is giving children enough time to play and clean up, as well as organizing the center materials carefully. Here are some ideas:

■ *Notify children well in advance.* Start cleanup in the block area sooner than other areas, and notify children that cleanup time is approaching so they can put the final touches on their creations.

■ *Acknowledge children's constructions.* Go over to the block area to view and discuss the buildings. Children will be less reluctant to dismantle a building if it has been noticed and appreciated.

■ *Assign tasks.* Assign certain items to individual children. Timmy can pick up all the triangles and Sarah all the single units. Marybeth gets the long blocks, while Joshua puts away all the accessories. Or give each child a certain number of blocks to pick up. Breaking cleanup into tiny tasks makes it seem less taxing.

■ *Use puppets for encouragement.* Having many blocks to put away may seem overwhelming to children. A puppet can encourage smiles while offering other kinds of special assistance.

■ *Use toy vehicles to transport blocks.* Suggest children use a wagon or large truck to load up blocks and "drive" to the shelves.

■ *Try an assembly line.* Children can hand blocks from one to another, with the last child placing them on the shelves. Encouraging this kind of cooperation is important and can be fun for kids.

■ *Keep it light.* Let kids make a "bulldozer" by using a large block to push smaller blocks over to the shelves. Or, from time to time, designate a child to be the block corner "inspector." After the area is cleaned up, ask the inspector to report on how it looks. Applaud the block cleaners whenever they pass inspection.

■ *Acknowledge children's efforts.* Even when cleanup is slow, try and stay calm by thanking those children who are picking up blocks and putting them away. Praise their neat arrangements, and help them to feel the satisfaction of a job well done.

ACTIVITY PLANS
FOR TWOS, THREES, FOURS, AND FIVES

ILLUSTRATIONS BY NICOLE RUBEL

USING THE ACTIVITY PLANS

Children create wondrous things with blocks when they are left to their own imaginations. Yet there may be times when children need a little spark to enhance their block experiences. For instance, your children may be ready for a new challenge or an unusual problem to solve. Or perhaps you are looking for creative ways that block play can enhance other aspects of your curriculum. The activity plans that follow offer many ways to introduce new ideas, props, or materials to children in the block area without inhibiting *their* ideas or play themes. Designed for children age 2-5, they are not intended to *replace* your children's own creative play, but rather enhance it with themes and play ideas that are appropriate to their developmental interests and abilities.

While encouraging children to creatively experiment with different concepts, the child-centered plans include a variety of suggestions that enable children to use blocks to express their ideas and feelings, expand their imaginations, and relate block-building themes to their own personal experiences.

UNDERSTANDING YOUR ROLE

You may be accustomed to primarily thinking of yourself as an observer in the block corner, allowing children to build and discover on their own. Therefore, the idea of using "activity plans" may raise new questions: What is my role? How much interaction is too much — or too little?

The plans have been designed to require a minimum of teacher intervention and direction. After an activity idea has been introduced with related props and materials, quiet observation of children at play is usually suggested. This gives them time to freely and creatively experiment with an idea or concept, making use of props and materials in their own way, as well as solve their own problems and make their own decisions.

As children play, you can look for appropriate times to comment on what you see, ask questions to clarify unfolding dramas, offer additional materials and props, and assist children with any problems they may have related to their constructions. In other words, think of yourself as an assistant who gives children time and space to make discoveries on their own, but who also tries to ensure that their discoveries and play experiences are rich and fulfilling.

GETTING THE MOST OUT OF THE ACTIVITY PLANS

While the activity plans have been written and designed for children age 2-5, these ages represent a wide range of developmental levels. Therefore, you may find that certain plans need to be adapted to meet the needs of your group. For example, if a plan seems too difficult for a group of children, look for ways to simplify the activity, so that children find the idea challenging and enjoyable without feeling overwhelmed. On the other hand, if you're a teacher of threes, and your children have had many experiences building with blocks, you may find that some ideas for fours and fives are appropriate (with modification) for your group. Naturally, the key is being aware of your children's abilities, then looking for ways to enhance their abilities, interests, and experiences with appropriate activities.

The format of the activity plans is simple and easy to follow. Each plan includes the following sections:

■ *Aim:* This section details the learning and developmental areas being emphasized and the value of the activity.

■ *Group Size:* The suggested group size is the optimum number of children participating in the activity at one given time. Naturally, you may adjust the number up or down as needed, but remember, block activities usually work best with small groups so that children have plenty of blocks available for their constructions.

■ *Materials:* This section suggests props, blocks, and additional materials needed for the activity. You may find that you will substitute, add, or subtract materials and props based on your children's abilities and what materials you have on hand.

■ *Getting Ready:* In this section, suggested ways to introduce the theme, concept, or idea to children are discussed. The open-ended questions suggested in this section can start them thinking about a topic and help you find out what they may already know about it. Brainstorming ideas, creating experience charts, or reading recommended stories help prepare and motivate children for the activity. During this time, when appropriate, children are encouraged to look for ways to cooperate with one another to build

group constructions. These discussions may be done with a large group at circle time or with a small group before they begin the activity.

■ *Begin:* This is the step-by-step "how-to" section of the block activity. There are suggestions for organizing and introducing materials, starting the activity, interacting with children throughout the activity, and bringing it to a close. Open-ended questions offer ways to help children discuss their ideas and develop their play themes as they engage in the activity.

■ *Remember:* This section offers developmental considerations to think about when planning the activity for your children. Also included are tips related to safety, clean-up, and suggested ways to extend a particular concept or theme into other learning areas. These suggestions may often include non-block activities such as art, dictated stories, graphs, or experience-chart ideas.

■ *Books:* The books recommended at the bottom of the page have been carefully selected to reinforce your children's block-building experiences. They can be read before the activity as a way to either introduce a new block-building idea or to provide pictures or examples that inspire children to build. The books can also reinforce your children's block-building experiences when used as a follow-up activity. Look for these books and others in your school or public library.

SHARING THE PLANS WITH OTHERS

To get the most out of the activity plans featured in this guide, make them available to the assistant teachers, aides, volunteers, parents, or other adults who may work in your room.

In doing so, you are communicating your philosophy by providing them with tips on how to plan and organize activities, as well as appropriate ways to interact with children during play.

USING THE ACTIVITY INDEX

The index on pages 78-79 lists the activity plans featured in this guide, along with the developmental areas and skills that each plan develops.

Use this "at-a-glance" index to:

■ quickly scan the developmental areas covered in the plans.

■ highlight specific skills a plan reinforces when talking to parents.

■ easily identify and locate activity plans that reinforce certain skills you want to enhance in children.

■ assist you in planning block experiences that offer children varied opportunities to develop a wide range of skills.

BLOCKS

Paint, blocks, and water — could your twos be any happier?

PAINT THE BLOCKS: WASH THEM CLEAN!

Aim: Children will gain practice in fine-motor and problem-solving skills as they paint and wash blocks of various sizes and shapes.

Group Size: Three to four children.

Materials: Water-based tempera paints and small brushes with short handles; newsprint; old wooden unit blocks of various shapes; dishpan with warm, sudsy water; sponges; and towels and smocks.

GETTING READY

Tape large sheets of newsprint to the floor and put out the blocks. Then invite three to four children to join you on the floor. Point out the blocks and allow children to hold and feel them. Ask, "How do they feel?" Discuss the various shapes and sizes of the blocks. "Carla is holding a round-shaped block, and Marcus is holding a rectangle." Build on their comments and ideas. Then you can explain: "Today we're going to paint these blocks, then wash them clean!"

BEGIN

Provide paintbrushes and sponges for children to use as painting tools. Observe children's efforts and comment on their painting. "Nicholas is painting his block blue. It's a blue triangle. Annie is making red and green dots on her block."

Look to see if children turn their blocks over, or if they only paint one side. You can paint along with them, turning your block from side to side to paint each surface. As children finish painting their blocks, encourage them to make prints with their blocks on the paper.

As the blocks dry, draw children's attention to how different the blocks look. "Look at all of these colorful blocks! I see a yellow rectangle and a green square. Does anyone see a blue triangle?"

Wash Them Clean!

Later in the day (or on another day), invite children to wash the blocks. Fill a dishpan or the water table with warm sudsy water. Provide sponges, cloths and brushes for scrubbing. Your twos will be fascinated to see the water turn colors as they clean the blocks. As they wash the blocks, comment on how clean the blocks look. Let them hold a block under a running faucet so that they can watch the paint gradually wash away. Ask, "Wow, where did the paint go?"

Note: Be aware that the paint may not wash off of the blocks completely. Consider setting aside one block of each shape from your set and reserving those just for this activity.

Remember

▪ Some twos may not like the messiness of this activity. These children may enjoy washing the blocks the other children have painted.

▪ Painting all sides of the blocks should not be expected of most twos. Allow them to paint as many sides as they wish.

BOOKS

Share these books about colors and painting with your twos.

▪ *Mouse Paint* by Ellen Stoll Walsh (Harcourt Brace Jovanovich)

▪ *Nice and Clean* by Anne Rockwell (Macmillan)

▪ *Colors* by Leo Lionni (Pantheon)

BLOCKS

Here's a guessing game to help your children learn more about the shapes and sizes of blocks.

FEELY BAG BLOCKS

Aim: Children will use the sense of touch and visual discrimination to match shapes.

Group Size: Two to three children.

Materials: Material bag large enough to hold two unit blocks and for a child to place a hand inside; and blocks of simple shapes, such as squares, rectangles, triangles, and cylinders.

GETTING READY

Gather two or three children together and set out the blocks. Allow the children to examine the blocks and explore how they feel and look. As the children are playing, comment on the shapes. "Kevin, I see you have a round block. It doesn't have any corners. How does it feel?"

BEGIN

After the children have had ample time to explore the blocks, introduce the feely bag. Let your children continue to play with the blocks, or watch, as you invite one child to play with you.

Place two different block shapes inside the bag. (Make sure they are easily distinguishable by touch. Try a triangle and a circle or a square and a cylinder.) Then hold up a block for everyone to see that matches one of the blocks in the bag.

Invite the child to place his or her hand in the bag and find the block that is like the one you are holding. If the child needs help, ask him or her to *feel* the block you are holding, while you comment. "Connie, this block has straight edges and sharp corners. Can you feel a shape in the bag that has sharp corners like this one?" Encourage the child to try and find the matching block in the bag.

Repeat this game using different-shaped blocks. Continue until each child has had a turn.

Remember
- Keep this game going by helping children feel successful. If a child picks out the wrong block, say something positive about the one she has chosen. Give her another turn, offering help if needed.
- Younger twos may need to put both hands inside the bag in order to feel the whole block shape.
- Older twos love to correct adults' mistakes. Have children take turns being the teacher and asking you to find the matching block. Make some "silly mistakes" and let the children try to catch them.

BOOKS
Use these books to continue the focus on shapes.

- *All Shapes and Sizes* by Shirley Hughes (Lothrop, Lee & Shepard)
- *Look Around: A Book About Shapes* by Leonard Fisher (Viking Penguin)
- *Shapes Shapes Shapes* by Tana Hoban (Greenwillow Books)

BLOCKS

Your twos will feel powerful making and lifting these giant-size lightweight blocks!

"MAKE AND PLAY" BOX BLOCKS

Aim: Children will use gross- and fine-motor skills as they construct and play with large blocks.
Group Size: Three to four children.
Materials: Empty disposable-diaper boxes; newspaper, masking tape, decorative self-stick paper; and scissors.

GETTING READY

Show children the empty diaper boxes, and examine them together. Be playful. Try putting the boxes over your heads or using them in games of peek-a-boo.

After children have had fun with the boxes, explain, "Today we're going to use these boxes to make our own blocks to play with. They will be very big, but I bet you'll be able to lift them."

BEGIN

Explain to children that first you'll need to stuff the boxes with crumpled paper. Show them how to wad the newspaper into balls, and stuff the paper inside the boxes. Draw their attention to the sounds the crumpling paper makes, and comment on their actions. "Liza, I can see that you're pushing the paper down inside the box. Do you hear the sound the paper makes?" Allow children to help you close the flaps on each box and tape them shut.

Do the same with the other boxes, letting those children who are interested continue to help. Later, cover each block with decorative self-stick paper. Let the children feel the sticky surface of the paper, then ask, "What else is sticky like this paper? Do your fingers ever get this sticky?"

Continue until you have plenty of blocks for a small group of twos.

Block Play

Young children don't often have a chance to lift, carry, and stack large objects. Help them enjoy the experience by allowing them to use the blocks on their own. Gather a small group and ask, "What can we do with these great big blocks?"

Observe children, then describe their actions. "Samantha is putting one big block on top of another big block. Now

she is putting another big block on top of those!"

Provide props such as cars, trucks, and other toys to enhance children's play.

Remember

▪ Twos may quickly tire of making the blocks. Consider making a few blocks at a time over several days, or making the balance of them yourself at another time.
▪ Inspire new play by engaging in parallel play next to the children. Talk about your construction and props and encourage children to talk about theirs.

BOOKS

Share these books about building.	▪ *Bam! Zoom! Bam! A Building Book* by Eve Merriam (Walker)	▪ *The Little Red House* by Norma Jean Sawicki (Lothrop, Lee & Shepard)	▪ *Over, Under & Through* by Tana Hoban (Macmillan)

BLOCKS

This beginning block-play activity is full of drama and excitement for your youngest toddlers.

BUILD & CRASH

Aim: Children will practice fine-motor skills and experiment with balance and cause and effect.
Group Size: One to two children.
Materials: Set of cardboard bricks; and toys such as small people, animals, and trucks.

IN ADVANCE

While observing children in the block corner, look to see if they start to stack blocks and then knock them down. Do they enjoy the excitement of it, or are some frustrated or frightened by it? Carpeting the area in a low-pile, indoor-outdoor carpet and using cardboard blocks can muffle the sound of falling blocks for twos frightened by the noise.

You might go over and start a game where you stack a few cardboard blocks and invite a child to keep stacking them with you. With younger twos, the game might be that you stack the blocks, and they knock them down. Before long they will start to make their own stacks of two or three blocks to knock over.

BEGIN

When you notice children starting to stack blocks and knocking them down on their own, you may want to help them balance one block on top of another. As children select blocks or props to stack, support their decisions by asking, "Which block will you put on next? OK, let's see what happens." Go with whatever the child suggests, even when you think the tower will topple. Keep adding blocks until the tower collapses. You can comment, "Look, they all fell down. Did you hear them fall? How did they sound? Shall we try another one?" Continue to build as long as the child is interested.

Later, suggest props such as cars, trucks, people, and animals for children to add to their tumbling towers.

Remember
▪ As children develop fine-motor skills, the pleasure of building a tower will grow to match the pleasure of knocking one down. Then you can suggest that they try to use blocks to build a tower that stays up.

▪ Establish safety rules for building and knocking down towers. Make sure there is enough space around each building so children will not be hit by falling blocks. Allow children to knock down only their own buildings.

BOOKS
Share these books about block building.	▪ *Kate's Box* by Kay Chorao (E.P. Dutton)	▪ *Panda the Builder* by Oda Taro (Rand McNally)	▪ *Tool Book* by Gail Gibbons (Holiday House)

BLOCKS

It's time to build stacks of blocks that reach taller and taller and ...

HOW HIGH?

Aim: Children will use gross-motor and cognitive skills to stack blocks and compare the height of their stacks to their own height.

Group Size: Two to four children.

Materials: Large cardboard-brick blocks or shoeboxes stuffed with newspaper, taped shut, and covered with self-stick paper.

GETTING READY

Provide or make 15-20 blocks and invite a few children to come to an open space and build with you. Talk about stacking and building. Build a stack of blocks, and say to your children that your stack is "this high" as you put your hand at the level of the highest block. Ask children to make their own stacks, and encourage them to build even higher by asking, "Can you put another block on top? Can you make your stack even higher?"

BEGIN

When a child has put several blocks on top of each other ask, "How high is your stack?" Then place your hand on the highest block to show how high the stack is and say, "It comes to here." Place your hand at the same level of the child's body and name the body part that the stack is even with. "You made your stack knee-high." Continue to ask the child to stack more and make the stack waist- or belly-high. As the child adds even more blocks, ask, "How high is your stack now?"

You can later challenge twos by asking, "Can you make a stack as high as your eyes? As high as the sky?"

Remember

▪ Some children may only want to stack the blocks and not talk about their heights. (Their verbal skills may be limited, or they may just be intent on stacking and balancing the blocks.) Respond to each child's individual style of participation.

▪ Some children may want to make stacks only to knock them down. Knocking down is a fun experience, so provide plenty of opportunities for this kind of play.

▪ Consider using various sizes of boxes. Use a very large block as a base so that stacks can reach even greater heights. (You can also begin stacks on a low table.)

BOOKS

| Share these books about getting bigger. | ▪ *When I Was a Baby* by Catherine Anholt (Little, Brown) | ▪ *See What I Can Do* by Patricia Linehan (Grosset & Dunlap) | ▪ *Barney Is Big* by Nicki Weiss (Puffin Books) |

BLOCKS

Twos enjoy creating rows of blocks placed end-to-end. Here's a way to turn their rows into expressways!

BUSY, BUSY ROADS

Aim: Children will use perceptual and creative thinking skills as they create surfaces for vehicles, people, and animals to travel on.

Group Size: Two to three children.

Materials: Wooden unit blocks, small vehicles, animals, and people.

GETTING READY

Read one of the books suggested below. Then put some toy vehicles in a bag. After the story, have children take turns selecting a vehicle from the bag. Encourage them to identify the vehicle and discuss the sound it makes. Then have them pretend to move their car or truck on a smooth road, then a bumpy road. After playing with the toys, tell them that the vehicles will be available in the block area.

BEGIN

Observe children's play and allow them ample time to play on their own. If you notice a child placing blocks end-to-end, you can say, "Gee, I see you have three blocks lined up here. I bet they would make a nice road to drive these cars and trucks on."

Allow children time to experiment with the "roads" and cars. Observe and comment on their dramatic involvement. You can ask, "That car is moving fast on your road. I wonder where it's going?"

Later, if your children are still interested, encourage them to make their roads longer and longer. As a child comes to the end of his or her road you can say, "Look, you're at the end of your road. Where will your bus go now? Can you make your road longer?"

As children gain more experience with the idea of roads and transportation, you may want to suggest they build garages and gas stations for their vehicles.

Remember

- Young twos especially enjoy lining up blocks horizontally end-to-end. They also stand them up vertically in rows. Try this activity when you notice your twos engaged in this type of play.
- You can introduce the idea of creating roads to your twos by quietly modeling it in the block area.
- Twos often have trouble sharing space and may need your help to build roads near each other. Make sure they ask first before driving on each other's roads.

BOOKS

Use these books to enhance the activity.	• *Bus Stop* by Nancy Hellen (Orchard)	• *Davy Goes Places* by Lois Lenski (Walck)	• *Gus the Bus* by Olga Cossi (Scholastic)

BLOCKS

Now your twos can pretend to be falling blocks while building a tower together!

THEY ALL FALL DOWN!

Aim: Children learn about balance as they cooperate to build a tower together.

Group Size: Four to five children.

Materials: Five or six wooden unit blocks and four large hollow or cardboard blocks.

GETTING READY

Allow children ample time to play in the block area independently before introducing this activity. Prior to cleanup time, collect some unit blocks and cardboard blocks and bring them to a large open space. Begin a tower by placing one block on top of another. Place the other blocks on the floor next to the stacked blocks. Then invite a few children to join you.

BEGIN

Point out the blocks to the children. Tell them that you have started a building and need their help to finish it. Explain that each child will have a chance to add a block to the tower. To begin, select one child to add a block to the stack. Then say, "Let's pretend to be little blocks while we join hands and sing this song." Walk around the blocks singing this chant to the tune of "Ring Around the Rosy."

> *The blocks are getting taller,*
> *The blocks are getting taller.*
> *Add one,*
> *Add one,*
> *Till they all fall down!*

At the end of the chant, the children all fall down, as in "Ring Around the Rosy." Now another child is selected to add a block, and the rhyme is repeated. As each child comes into the circle to add a block, talk about the block he or she selects. "Let's see which block Jamie will pick. She picked out a big block. Now she's putting it on top of the little block. Let's see what happens." Repeat the rhyme and continue until each child has a turn or until the stack falls down. Then start again!

At cleanup time, have each child select two blocks to put away.

Remember

▪ This activity may be better suited for older twos who have begun to stack blocks and build towers — and who will enjoy seeing the blocks come down. Remember, some children may be frightened by the tumbling.

▪ Help children understand that it's okay (and even more fun) for the tower to fall, so that individual children aren't frustrated when it falls.

BOOKS

Here are some books to keep your twos moving.

▪ *Piggyback Songs for Infants and Toddlers* by Jean Warren (Warren Publishing)

▪ *Wee Sing & Play* by Pamela Beall and Susan Nipp (Price, Stern, Sloan)

▪ *Your Baby Needs Music* by Barbara Cass-Beggs (St. Martins Press)

BLOCKS

Twos love to stick objects through holes. Here's a way to try this favorite activity with blocks.

BLOCK SHAPE SORTERS

Aim: Children will observe, classify, and sort, as well as use fine-motor skills, to insert blocks of different sizes and shapes through holes in a box.
Group Size: Two or three children.
Materials: Four shapes of wooden unit blocks such as rectangles, squares, triangles, and cylinders; four large cardboard boxes; marking pen; sharp knife; and drawing paper.

IN ADVANCE
Twos enjoy watching things being constructed, so let interested children observe you preparing the sorting boxes,

keeping the knife safely out of their reach at all times. Start with one box and one shape. Turn the box upside down and use the open flaps for retrieving the blocks from inside. Trace the shape on the bottom (now top) of the box. Then use the knife to carefully cut along the outline, removing the cardboard cutout to leave a hole. Repeat with the other boxes and shapes — making one box for each shape.

BEGIN
Give each child the same-shaped block and encourage them to examine its shape. Now put out the sorting box of the same shape and say, "All of your blocks will fit through the hole in this box. See, the blocks and the hole are the same shape."(Point to the block and hole.) Allow each child to take a turn putting the block in the hole.

Help children position the block just right to fit through the hole in the box. Now try another block and box and let them try it on their own.

As children catch on, offer two shapes, such as squares and triangles, and the two corresponding boxes. Give each child a few blocks of each shape. Can they figure out which box to put the blocks in?

As children engage in this sorting activity, talk about the shapes they are handling. "That's a triangle block, Randa. Can you find the box with the triangle cutout? Keith has a square-shaped block. Let's see if he can find the box with the square shape on it." When the challenge of sorting two block shapes gets easy, add more shapes.

Remember
- Twos are still gaining physical knowledge of blocks — their sizes, weights, and shapes. Activities like these help twos learn more about these concepts.
- By observing, you will know when to add more shapes. You may only want to do one at a time with some children.
- As children become more experienced, consider making a shape-sorting box with several differently shaped holes in the same box.

BOOKS

Here are some good books about shapes.	▪ *Holes* by Joan Rahn (Houghton Mifflin)	▪ *Holes & Peeks* by Ann Jonas (Greenwillow Books)	▪ *Shapes, Shapes, Shapes* by Tana Hoban (Greenwillow Books)

BLOCKS

Your children will enjoy filling and emptying these containers with blocks.

TOTE THOSE BLOCKS

Aim: Children will gain a physical knowledge of blocks as they put them inside different containers and carry them around.

Group Size: Two to four children.

Materials: Wooden unit blocks of various shapes and sizes; a variety of containers with handles such as shopping bags, baskets, large purses, small suitcases, and small wagons; and two large boxes.

GETTING READY

Gather a few children around the various containers. Let the children examine the containers and talk about the kinds of things we carry in them. Then say, "Look around the classroom. What are some things we can put in this suitcase? What about this bag? This pocketbook?"

Then ask, "Do you think we can put blocks in these containers and carry them around? Let's see." Then tell the children that the containers will be in the block area for them to try out.

BEGIN

Observe to see how children use the various containers with the blocks. The youngest children are learning about blocks simply by feeling how heavy they are and how much space they take up. Attach language labels as appropriate. "Jeremy put all the small blocks in his bag."

While children are playing, place a large empty box on the opposite side of the room. Invite children who have filled up a container to carry their blocks over and dump them out in the box across the room. You can say, "Gee, Jerry, you have a lot of blocks in that wagon. I bet they could fill up that box over there. Do you want to try and see?" Make similar suggestions to other children, and observe them as they carry the blocks and dump them in the box. As children unload their blocks, describe the blocks they brought over: "Let's see, Jon, you have two long blocks, a triangular one, and five little square ones. You found a lot of blocks with different shapes."

As cleanup time approaches, suggest that each child use a different container to tote the blocks back to the block area and put them away!

Remember

▪ Twos love counting activities. Encourage them to "help" you count, as they load and unload.

▪ Older twos will enjoy using these activities in their dramatic play, pretending to deliver packages, groceries, or materials to a construction site.

BOOKS

| Here are some stories about moving people and things. | ▪ *Moving* by Fred Rogers (Putnam Publishing Group) | ▪ *Now We Can Go* by Ann Jonas (Greenwillow Books) | ▪ *Sam's Wagon* by Barbro Lindgren (William Morrow & Co.) |

BLOCKS

Your twos will practice taking turns as they build a structure with you.

YOU ADD ONE, AND I'LL ADD ONE

Aim: Children will gain practice in using words that describe location and spatial relationships as they tell you where to place blocks.

Group Size: One child at a time.

Materials: Wooden unit blocks or cardboard blocks, and block toys and accessories.

IN ADVANCE

This is a good activity for a new child or for a child who seldom plays with blocks. It's also a good way to introduce older twos to the concept of taking turns. Invite the child to play with you in the block area. Tell him or her, "Let's build something together!"

BEGIN

Once in the block area, allow the child to take the lead and direct you where to put the blocks. You can begin by saying, "You pick a block first and put it on the floor. You picked a long rectangular block. Now it is my turn to add a block." After you select the block, ask, "Where would you like me to put this block?" Let the child direct you where to put the block each time it is your turn. Then say, "Now it is your turn again."

If the child simply points to a location for the block, you can supply the words. "You want me to put my block behind this round one?" Or if a child is slow to respond, give her some time to think then say, "Would you like it on top of this block? Or here?" pointing to various locations.

Describe the building as it takes shape. "This building has lots of rooms. What do you think we could put in them? What kind of building could this be?" Allow the child time to make some suggestions. Then provide block people, animals, or vehicles, and allow the child to direct their placement. Express pleasure at working together. "This is fun, building together and taking turns, isn't it?"

Remember

▪ Taking turns is a difficult concept to master for two-year-olds. It's easier and more fun with an adult. With lots of practice, children might eventually enjoy playing this game

with other children.

▪ With this activity especially, the child should feel that she is in control. Accept all of a child's suggestions, even if it means the structure may topple over.

BOOKS

These books offer other activities to do with twos.

▪ *Active Learning for Twos* by Debby Cryer, Thelma Harms and Beth Bourland (Addison-Wesley)

▪ *Things to Do With Toddlers and Twos* by Karen Miller (Telshare)

▪ *Celebrate!* by Tamara Hunt and Nancy Renfro (Nancy Renfro Studios)

BLOCKS

The block corner is the perfect place for an impromptu game of bowling.

LET'S GO BLOCK BOWLING

Aim: Children will use eye-hand coordination, gross-motor, and social skills as they bowl with blocks.
Group Size: Three to four children.
Materials: Unit blocks and cardboard or milk-carton blocks, a rubber ball, and masking tape.

GETTING READY

Take a few minutes to talk about bowling. Invite children to tell about any experiences they have had with bowling. Perhaps they have gone bowling with their parents or watched others bowl. Ask, "What do people do when they bowl? What happens in the game? What do the players try to do?" As you talk about the game, help children become familiar with words such as *pins*, *alley*, and *strike*.

BEGIN

Gather a small group of children in the block area and say, "We can make a bowling alley right here in our block area. What type of blocks should we use for our bowling pins?" Help children choose which blocks to use. (Try starting out with about five blocks. Add more as their aim improves.) Next, have them select a starting line for rolling the ball. Put a strip of tape on the floor to mark the line. Use another piece of tape at the other end to show where the blocks should stand.

Time to Play

Take turns standing behind the starting line and rolling the ball into the blocks. Give the children as many tries as they need to knock them all down. Encourage all of them to add their support and cheers. Here's a cheer to say while you bowl:

> *Stand them up.*
> *Roll the ball.*
> *Knock them down.*
> *See them fall!*

Remember

- Adjust the game to fit the needs of individual children. Some children may need a larger ball or a shorter distance to be successful.
- As children get better at the game, add more blocks or accessories to the blocks being knocked down.
- While children wait for their turns, let them be "pin setters" and set up the blocks for the next player.

BOOKS

| The following are books about other toys threes enjoy. | ▪ *Things I Like to Play With* by Harriet Ziefert (Simon & Schuster) | ▪ *Harriet at Play* by Betsy and Giulio Maestro (Crown) | ▪ *Games* by Rodney Peppe (Viking Penguin) |

BLOCKS

Children love musical games. Here are some to try with blocks.

MUSICAL BLOCKS

Aim: Children will use listening and gross-motor skills as they play a block game.

Group Size: Four to five children.

Materials: A set of blocks, a record or cassette player, and instrumental music for movement.

GETTING READY

At group time, invite children to choose a favorite musical selection. Put on the record or tape, and move with children to the beat. Then all of a sudden (very dramatically) turn off the music and stand very still. Notice which children imitate you. Explain that in this game, everyone listens very closely to the music, and when it stops their bodies stop, too.

BEGIN

After children are familiar with the listening game, bring a record or cassette player to the block area during cleanup time. Explain that each time the music plays, everyone moves to it, and each time it stops, it's time to put the blocks away. Continue playing until all blocks are in their proper spaces. Soon putting blocks away will be as popular as building with them!

Remember

▪ Young threes can begin with an easier, faster version of this game, in which the whole group can participate. During regular cleanup time, play music while they work. When the music stops, everyone takes a break. Cleanup resumes when the music plays, etc.

BOOKS

Here are some books to keep your children moving.

▪ *Busy Feet* by Elizabeth Watson (Standard Publishing Company)

▪ *Sounds My Feet Make* by Arlene Blanchard (Random House)

▪ *Freckly Feet and Itchy Knees* by Michael Rosen (Doubleday)

BLOCKS

Dramatic play and creative thinking begin when your children bring an old box to life with blocks!

APPLIANCE BOX STRUCTURES

Aim: Children will use creative-thinking and problem-solving skills, as well as social skills, in dramatic play with blocks.

Group Size: Four to five children.

Materials: A large appliance box (refrigerator or washing machine); unit and cardboard blocks; sharp knife; paints, brushes, and construction paper; and assorted art materials.

GETTING READY

Gather a group of children around the appliance box. Ask, "What do you think came in this box? How could we change it to make something we could play in?" Turn the box on its side and ask, "What could it be if we used it this way? Or, standing upright, "What could it be now?" List children's suggestions on chart paper, adding simple pictures to illustrate the ideas. Ask the group to choose the idea they like best. Some possible ideas might be a house, castle or other building; a tunnel; a bus, train, boat or other vehicle; a rocket ship; or a dinosaur.

BEGIN

Help the children decide what materials will be needed to change the box. Take your cues from the children, and let them decide where openings should go. Cut any doors, windows or other openings they suggest. (Keep the knife out of their reach at all times.) Then give them art materials and allow them to paint and decorate the box.

Add the Blocks

When the box is dry, gather the children around and ask, "Now, how can we add blocks to make this more fun to play with? Could we use them to make sidewalks or roads or fences or furniture? What do you think?" Help them assemble the blocks and accessories needed to complete the project.

The appliance box now becomes the focus for block building and creative play. For example, the box with both ends cut off functions nicely as a tunnel. Children can use blocks to build roads and fences leading up to it, then drive toy trucks through it!

Remember

▪ Some children may be afraid to play inside the box. Help them become more comfortable by suggesting games where they can peek in windows or go in and out.

▪ Threes may not be able to reach a consensus on what to build. Tell them you will start out with one idea, and they can try out more on other days.

▪ Create a system to help limit the number of children allowed in the box at a time.

BOOKS

Continue the focus on boxes and building with these books.

▪ *Boxes, Boxes* by Leonard Fisher (Viking Kestrel)

▪ *Evan's Corner* by Elizabeth Hill (Harper & Row)

▪ *Inside, Outside, Upside Down* by Stan Berenstain (Random House)

BLOCKS

Children learn about a variety of animals while creating homes for them.

LET'S BUILD A ZOO!

Aim: Children will use creative-thinking, problem-solving, and perceptual skills as they use blocks to create homes for zoo animals.

Group Size: One to three children at a time.

Materials: Wooden unit blocks, cardboard or milk-carton blocks; and small plastic, wooden, and stuffed animals.

IN ADVANCE

An ideal way to introduce this activity is with a field trip to a zoo. If that's not possible, use pictures from favorite animal books as a springboard for small group discussion. You can also display pictures of animals in the block area.

GETTING READY

Prior to bringing the children together, place some plastic and stuffed animals on the floor of the block area. During group time, read a story about the zoo to children. After the story, encourage children to talk about their experiences at the zoo. Also have children talk about any pets or other experiences with animals they may have had.

Then invite some children to come to the block area for a building activity.

BEGIN

When children arrive in the block area, point out the animals on the floor. Say, "Look at all of these animals. I wonder what we can do with them?" Then encourage children to identify some of the animals, what they eat, and where they live. Then say, "Maybe we could build our own zoo!"

Encourage the children to think of the kinds of homes the animals would like. Point out the sizes of the animals. Which animals would need a big space to live in, and which could live in smaller spaces?

Help children select the blocks they need to get started. Provide additional accessories and materials, such as people, small trees, green paper for grass, or blue paper for water, and let children know they are available. Encourage children to create the additional accessories they need from clay or playdough, paper, and Popsicle sticks.

Notice when children make enclosures and comment on

them. "Mellie, you're building a big fence. Which animals will live there? What else do you think they would like?"

Later, children may want to dictate stories about the zoo. Record their stories on an experience chart, and invite other children to come visit the zoo.

Remember

- Young threes may still play parallel to one another. However, this activity can lead children into cooperative play where they share ideas and work together.
- Allow children to construct the animals' homes according to their own play themes and ideas, rather than stressing that any of their homes should look a certain way.
- Encourage children to talk about their animal homes informally and at group sharing times. Older threes might like to dictate signs or stories and conduct guided "tours."

BOOKS

| Use these stories about animals to add to the fun. | ▪ *A House Is a House for Me* by Mary Ann Hoberman (Viking Penguin) | ▪ *Dick Bruna's Animal Book* by Dick Bruna (Methuen) | ▪ *What's That Size?* by Kate Petty (Franklin Watts) |

BLOCKS

Double the fun indoors or out by combining two of your children's favorite play materials.

BLOCKS IN THE SANDBOX!

Aim: Children will use problem-solving, creative-thinking, fine- and gross-motor skills, as they build with blocks in the sandbox.

Group Size: Three or four children.

Materials: Wooden unit or table blocks; indoor or outdoor sandbox; sand toys; block accessories, such as small vehicles, people, and animals; and a large wagon for transporting blocks.

GETTING READY

Talk about building with blocks in the sandbox. Ask, "What would it be like if we used our blocks in the sandbox? What could we build?" Invite children to share their ideas. Then ask, "Do you think it would be harder or easier to build in sand? Let's try it and see."

BEGIN

Gather a small group of children in the block area. Show them the wagon, and suggest that they fill it carefully with the blocks they want to use.

After the children have unloaded the blocks, let them play freely with the blocks and accessories in the sand. Watch as they discover how to anchor the blocks in the sand to make them stand up. Ask, "Sharon, how did you figure out how to make that block stand up? Jason, you're pushing that block along and clearing away the sand. What are you making?" Allow the children the freedom to experiment with this combination.

At the end of play time, have the children clean the sand off the blocks with paper towels. As they do, ask them to describe how the blocks feel. Then load up the blocks and bring them back indoors to the block area.

Extend the experience another day by asking children to think of accessories, such as animals, vehicles, and containers, to add to their play. Also add accessories from nature such as shells, sticks, and pine cones.

Remember

▪ Introduce this activity when children have had plenty of experience playing with sand and with blocks separately.

▪ If everyone clamors for a turn at this activity, reassure children that there will be plenty of opportunities for them to take part in this play.

▪ If a wagon isn't available, blocks can be shuttled in shopping bags, baskets, large cars and trucks, and cardboard or plastic cartons.

BOOKS

| These beach books will add to the joy of sand and block play. | ▪ *At the Beach* by Anne Rockwell (Macmillan) | ▪ *Dinosaur Beach* by Liza Donnelly (Scholastic) | ▪ *Discovering Sea Shells* by Douglas Florian (Charles Scribner's Sons) |

BLOCKS

The child is the leader and you follow in this block activity.

FOLLOW THE LEADER WITH BLOCKS!

Aim: Children will observe the size, shape, and location of blocks, as well as gain practice in taking turns.

Group Size: One child at a time.

Materials: A supply of various shapes and sizes of unit or table blocks, at least two of each shape.

GETTING READY

Invite a child to join you in the block area or join a child who is already there. Say, "Today I would like to build what you build with blocks. You can be the teacher, and tell me what to do!" (Your children will enjoy the sense of power they get from telling you what to do.)

Have the child select a collection of blocks to use. As the child selects his or her blocks, you select the same ones. Try and collect about 7-10 pairs of identical blocks.

BEGIN

Sort your blocks into separate piles and suggest that the child begin to build. One at a time, as he selects and uses a block, you select the same one. Place and position your block in the way that the child does. Every once in a while, encourage him to look at the two structures to see if they are still the same. You can ask, "Is mine just like yours?"

You can also describe the blocks you're using as you place them. "Now I'm placing this triangle on top of this big block just like you." For fun you can pick up a wrong block to see if he catches you. If not, ask, "Do I have the right block?" Another day, you can reverse roles and have the child copy you.

Remember

- Younger children may be unable to verbalize their actions. Help build vocabulary by describing their choices of blocks and locations.
- Limit the number of blocks to keep the activity simple.
- After playing this game with you, older threes may enjoy playing it with a friend. Encourage them to compare their buildings when they are finished. Are they exactly the same?

BOOKS

Use these books to enhance the experience.

- *Becca Backward, Becca Frontward* by Bruce McMillan (Lothrop, Lee & Shepard)

- *Opposites* by Rosalinda Kightley (Little, Brown)

- *I Can Build a House* by Shigeo Watanabe (Philomel Books)

BLOCKS

Threes love to hide and then surprise you. Now they can create their very own little hideaways with blocks.

MY HIDEAWAY

Aim: Children will use their imaginations and visual perception skills as they construct block hideaways that they can fit inside.

Group Size: Two to three children.

Materials: Large blocks, such as cardboard bricks, milk-carton blocks, or vinyl-covered foam blocks; sheets or blankets; and scrap construction paper.

GETTING READY

Help children start thinking about hiding and hiding places by playing a quick game of hide and seek. After the game, talk about some of the places they used for hiding. Encourage children to share why they selected certain places. Then say, "Let's play hide-and-seek with blocks. I bet each of you could make a hiding place with blocks! Would you like to try?"

BEGIN

Before children begin, show them the additional accessories available to them. These may include blankets or sheets, cardboard or plastic cartons, and large sheets of cardboard. Let them know that they can use these materials to create their hideaways. Using blocks as markers, help each child mark off how much space he or she will need to make a hideaway that will accommodate his size.

Now let the children freely play and experiment, using the blocks and other materials to create their hiding places. From time to time, support their efforts by observing their actions and making comments. "How high do you think your walls will be? How will you get in and out?"

Later, have an "open house" and allow children to give "guided tours" of their hideaways. Children may also enjoy a game of hide-and-seek and use their hideaways as hiding spaces. (For safety's sake, make sure these activities are closely supervised.)

Remember

▪ It can be difficult for three-year-olds to figure out how large to make their structures because they cannot see the length of their bodies as they build. They will need your

help at this early stage.

▪ Children who are ready for cooperative play might enjoy working in pairs, helping each other build.

▪ Since these buildings may fall during a game of hide-and-seek, an alternative might be for children to help you construct special ones for the game.

BOOKS

| Share these books about moving and hiding. | ▪ *We Hide, You Seek* by Jose Aruego (Greenwillow Books) | ▪ *Over, Under & Through* by Tana Hoban (Macmillan) | ▪ *Where's Spot?* by Eric Hill (Putnam Publishing Group) |

BLOCKS

A great activity for a rainy day when everyone needs a lift.

SHINING SILVER SKYSCRAPERS

Aim: Children will gain fine-motor practice as they wrap blocks with foil and use their imagination as they build and play with light in different ways.

Group Size: Three to four children.

Materials: Unit blocks; a roll of aluminum foil; flashlights; and transparent colored plastic report covers or colored cellophane.

GETTING READY

Show children the aluminum foil. Do they know what it is? What is it used for? Give each child a small piece to play with. Help children notice how the foil changes its shape when they bend or fold it. Tear off a piece, and let children watch you wrap a block in the foil. Now tear off pieces of foil of appropriate size and invite the children to wrap some blocks.

BEGIN

When the children have covered a number of blocks with the foil, invite them to build something with the shiny blocks. Observe them as they build. Ask, "How do the silver blocks feel? What is it like to use them?" Encourage the children to talk about the blocks while building. Observe them to see what kind of creations these silver blocks inspire.

Blocks in the Spotlight

When the children have finished building, darken the room and bring out a flashlight for each child. Let them shine their flashlights on their constructions. Point out how the light is reflected off of their buildings. You can also point out the shapes and sizes of the shadows on the wall.

Later, bring out some transparent colored plastic or cellophane. Invite children to shine their flashlights through the colors onto the blocks. How do they look now? Can they make the colors mix? Write down any stories that emerge!

Remember

▪ Some children may be afraid of the dark. Perhaps these children can build under a table with a blanket draped over it. Then they can shine the flashlight into the darkened space.

▪ Your children may quickly tire of wrapping the blocks. Wrap a number of them in advance so that they are ready for play when your children are.

BOOKS

| Here are some books about wrapping things up. | ▪ *The Toy Trumpet* by Ann Grifalconi (Bobbs-Merrill) | ▪ *Max's Toys* by Rosemary Wells (Dial Books) | ▪ *Doll and Drum* by Sue Tarsky (Simon & Schuster) |

BLOCKS

Pillows, stuffed animals, and blankets in the block area add a soft touch while inspiring new play themes.

CREATING SOFT SPOTS WITH BLOCKS

Aim: Children will use their creative-thinking skills and sense of touch as they are challenged to use a variety of "soft" accessories with blocks.

Group Size: Four to six children

Materials: An assortment of soft things such as fabric pieces of different sizes, colors, and textures; small swatches of upholstery samples; large scarves, rug remnants, pillows, stuffed animals, tablecloths, blankets, and towels; and unit blocks or hollow blocks.

GETTING READY

Three-year-olds greatly enjoy dramatic play of all types. Soft items like fabric samples, rug remnants, pillows, and stuffed animals are likely to bring dramatic play into your block area and help children create new settings and roles.

Tell children that you have soft things for them to feel. Let them examine and play with the fabric pieces, pillows, and stuffed animals during circle time, and practice folding the fabric to change its size and shape. Encourage them to hug the pillows and animals and describe how they feel.

Talk about the color and texture of each. Offer descriptive words such as *soft*, *rough*, *bumpy*, *smooth*, etc. "Mark has some dark-green velvet. How does it feel, Mark?" Or, "Kira

is holding a pillow. When do you use a pillow, Kira?" Then ask, "How do you think we could use these things in the block area? What could we build with them?"

BEGIN

Simply place the fabric, rug pieces, pillows, and stuffed animals in the block corner, and watch to see how children use them with the blocks. Do they spread the fabric out and build on top of it or drape it over the buildings? Do the pillows become beds for the stuffed animals to sleep on?

Later encourage children to describe how they have incorporated the accessories into their structures.

Remember

▪ Threes sometimes find it hard to share new materials. Be sure to have several objects of each type available.

▪ Too many new materials at once can be overstimulating. Consider putting out only some of the items and adding more later, as needs arise or as interest wanes.

▪ As you observe children working, look for opportunities to expand their dramatic play.

BOOKS

| Here are some touch and texture books to share at storytime. | ▪ *My Bunny Feels Soft* by Charlotte Steiner (Alfred A. Knopf) | ▪ *Pat the Bunny* by Dorothy Kurnhardt (Golden Press) | ▪ *Find Out by Touching* by Paul Showers (Thomas Y. Crowell) |

BLOCKS

Your threes will be amazed at the size of the shadows they cast with blocks!

CASTING SHADOWS IN THE GREAT OUTDOORS

Aim: Children experiment with shadows and shapes as they build with blocks outside.

Group Size: Two to three children.

Materials: An assortment of unit or cardboard blocks, chalk, a wagon, a large open space for building, and a plastic tablecloth (optional).

GETTING READY

During circle time, talk about all of the usual activities your children take part in outdoors. Have them brainstorm

all of the things they enjoy doing.

Then ask, "Have you ever seen your shadow when playing outside? What does it look like?" Allow children time to respond.

Then ask, "What if we took some of our blocks outdoors and built towers with them? Would the blocks have shadows, too?" Allow children to respond to the questions and share their ideas.

End circle time by reading one of the books suggested below.

BEGIN

When it's time for outdoor play, have children load up the blocks in a wagon, shopping bag, or cardboard box. Once you're outdoors, have interested children go with you on a shadow hunt. Encourage them to look for places where they can easily find their own shadows. This place will be their building spot.

When you find the spot, point out the children's shadows to them. Can they make their shadows bigger and smaller?

Using the chalk, mark off an area for block play. Then have children unload the blocks and start to build. As their towers get taller and taller, point out how much taller the shadows are. Let them experiment to see which blocks make larger shadows and which make smaller ones.

Before the children take down their towers, trace around them using the chalk, and write the children's names on each one.

Remember

• Select an outdoor location with a flat surface to easily see and trace shadows. Keep safety in mind and stay away from high traffic areas. If the sun is strong, remember sunscreen.

• Younger threes will need help tracing their shadows. Older threes can probably do it on their own.

• Provide older threes with mural paper on which to trace their shadows. They can use markers or paints to color them in, and dictate stories about them.

BOOKS

| Here are some books that cast big shadows, too. | ▪ *What Makes a Shadow?* by Clyde Bulla (Harper & Row) | ▪ *Shadows* by Taro Gomi (Heian International) | ▪ *Science Fun With a Flashlight* by Herman and Nina Schneider (McGraw-Hill) |

BLOCKS

Your children will enjoy creating a whole houseful of furniture in your block area.

MAKING BLOCK FURNITURE

Aim: Children will use creative-thinking, planning, and problem-solving skills as they use blocks to create furniture.

Group Size: Four or five children.

Materials: Hollow blocks or large cardboard blocks; old, clean sheets; blankets; drapes or slip covers; props from the dramatic-play area; and pictures of furniture from catalogs or weekly sales circulars.

GETTING READY

Share pictures of furniture, and talk about different rooms in houses and the furniture that is found in them. Brainstorm, with your children, a list of all the different kinds of furniture found in a home.

BEGIN

Look over the list of furniture pieces your children brainstormed earlier. Ask children to choose which pieces they would like to build out of blocks. Small groups of children may want to work together.

As children begin, ask problem-solving questions such as, "Can you build a couch big enough for two people to sit on? A table and chairs? A bed for a baby?" Then give children time to experiment with different ways to construct their ideas.

You might want to suggest they try adding large sheets of cloth, table cloths, or blankets to drape over the furniture. When the children feel their furniture is complete, encourage them to add props from the dramatic-play area to enhance their play.

If the furniture seems sturdy enough, you may want to suggest that the day's snack be served in this new addition to the classroom!

Remember

▪ Your children may not want to dismantle the furniture right away. If you have room, consider leaving it up as long as the children seem interested. They may want to write stories about the rooms or continue to expand on their play.

▪ Use these ideas to enhance children's ongoing pretend play. At appropriate moments, suggest they build any furniture they need either in or near the dramatic-play area.

▪ Accept and encourage children to follow their own ideas. When discussing homes and furniture, be sensitive to children's varied experiences. (Remember, it's not uncommon to find a bed or bathtub in the kitchen.)

BOOKS

Use these books to start some good conversations about homes and furniture.	▪ *My House* by Zokeisha (Simon & Schuster)	▪ *My Kitchen* by Harlow Rockwell (Greenwillow Books)	▪ *Table and Chair* by Sue Tarsky (Simon & Schuster)

BLOCKS

Your children will be "amazed" at the fun and excitement this activity generates!

MAZES AND BALLS

Aim: Children will use fine- and gross-motor skills as they plan, construct, and play with a large maze.

Group Size: Four or five children.

Materials: Unit, hollow, or large table blocks; Ping-Pong balls; small rubber balls; large plastic straws; thick pencils; chalk; and a timer or watch (optional).

IN ADVANCE

Draw a simple maze on a sheet of mural paper or large sheets of construction paper taped together.

GETTING READY

Show children the maze. Ask them if they have ever seen or used one before. Explain that a maze is a kind of puzzle

where players have to find their way to get from one part of it to another. With your finger, demonstrate how to go through the maze you created. Then, give a few children a chance to work their way through the maze. (Be sure to explain that a solid line is a "wall" that you can't go through to reach the goal.)

BEGIN

Gather children together in the block area and say, "We can build a maze out of blocks." Explain that together you're going to build a maze using unit blocks big enough to blow a Ping-Pong ball through. Show children the picture of the simple maze again, and point out how it is like a path or a trail. Offer a child a piece of chalk and invite him or her to draw a crooked path on the floor. Then ask a few volunteers to build a wall of blocks on the chalk line.

Next ask, "How can we build this maze so that the Ping-Pong ball won't roll out of it?" Help children construct a second wall of blocks to form an alley to roll the ball through. Show children how to add corners and turns to make the maze more challenging.

Encourage children to work cooperatively on the maze until it fills up the entire block area.

Try It Out!

When the maze is complete, have children take turns blowing a Ping-Pong ball around on the floor using straws. (Allow time for them to experiment until they find the best angle to blow the ball.) Then place the ball at the beginning of the maze and invite one child at a time to blow the ball through the maze.

Later, your children might like to make small mazes for their friends to try.

Remember

▪ Children may need to trace the chalk line with their fingers a few times to gain a better understanding of where to build.

▪ Young fours may need practice with the maze before using the Ping-Pong balls. Have them move small vehicles, animals, or people through the maze first.

BOOKS

| Add these books to your circle time selections. | ▪ *Catch That Hat* by Emma Chichester Clark (Little, Brown) | ▪ *The Great 200 Hunt* by Pippa Unwin (Doubleday) | ▪ *Jesse Builds a Road* by Laurence Pringle (Macmillan) |

BLOCKS

Motivate your children with these challenging constructions.

"STARTER" BUILDINGS

Aim: Children will use problem-solving and creative thinking skills as they add to existing block structures.
Group Size: Three or four children.
Materials: Unit blocks and cardboard blocks, and a Polaroid camera and film (optional).

IN ADVANCE

Before children arrive, construct a few starter buildings in the block area. A "starter" building is a simple unfinished structure to which children can add. As children complete them they are practicing creative problem-solving.

GETTING READY

Talk about block building. Ask, "What kinds of structures have you been building in the block area? What new kinds of buildings would you like to make?" As children make suggestions record them on a rebus chart, and display it in the block area for inspiration.

BEGIN

Take two or three children over to the "starter" buildings in the block area. Talk about the way they look and how they have been constructed. To help children begin to build you can ask, "What can you add to these constructions? What do you think they could be?" If possible, let the children use the instant camera to take a "before" photograph of the building before they change it.

Allow children ample time to add different blocks and props to the structures. Encourage them to point out the additions they have made to the buildings. How have the buildings changed? Have they gotten taller? More spread out? What accessories have been added?

When children have finished building, you can record their responses on an experience chart. Let them take photos of their completed constructions. Display the "before" and "after" pictures along with their comments.

Remember

▪ After completing these starter buildings, encourage children to create starter buildings for each other to complete.

▪ Skilled block builders who enjoyed this activity might like to try working with more complex starter buildings. Set up structures of unusual shapes, or challenge children to add doors, a roof, or a second floor.
▪ Plan related discussions and experiences. Ask children if they have ever seen buildings being renovated or having additions built on. If possible, take a trip to see one.

BOOKS

These books feature interesting buildings and stories for children.	▪ *Changes, Changes* by Pat Hutchins (Macmillan)	▪ *I Can Build a House* by Shigeo Watanabe (Philomel Books)	▪ *Airport* by Byron Barton (Thomas Y. Crowell)

BLOCKS

Help children practice patterning with a new twist!

PATTERNING WITH BLOCKS

Aim: Children will use patterning, observing, and creative-thinking skills as they create patterns with blocks.

Group Size: Four or five children.

Materials: Unit, table, or colored blocks; pre-cut construction paper shapes; drawing paper; glue; objects that have a simple observable pattern on them such as a sweater, scarf, or other material; and floor tiles or wallpaper samples.

GETTING READY

Introduce the concept of patterning by showing children objects that have recognizable patterns such as a striped scarf, checkered material, etc. Together, talk about the patterns. Point out the ways they repeat themselves. Encourage children to look at each other's clothes to see if anyone is wearing a repeating pattern.

Now play a simple "people pattern" game to help children experience the concept. First make a "boy/girl/boy/girl" pat-

tern. Invite a few children to line up in front of the group and ask the others to say the "boy/girl" pattern. Ask, "What would come next in the pattern? A boy or a girl?" Have children continue to add to the pattern. Try another people pattern such as "stand/sit/stand/sit" or "front/back/front/back." With each pattern encourage children to say or chant it back and forth and ask, "What comes next?"

BEGIN

Now have children try to create patterns with blocks. Use a small set of blocks with only a few shapes and choose two. Show children a simple two-block pattern, such as "square/triangle/square/triangle." Encourage children to continue the pattern.

Next try three-part patterns. This time, ask children to choose three different shapes or colored blocks and create their own patterns. Help them see that the same order of colors or shapes should be repeated over and over.

Encourage children to say, chant, or sing their patterns as they build them. This auditory clue helps children incorporate the pattern concept. Children seem to enjoy the repetitive nature of the chanting,

If children are ready for a challenge, have them create a pattern "wall" with blocks. Show them how a pattern can be built into one long continuous wall. Ask, "How long can you build your pattern wall? What is your pattern?"

Remember

▪ Introduce this concept gradually, especially to younger fours. You might do people patterns one day, and block patterns another day. Provide lots of time and experience for children to practice the concept before having them create the pattern walls.

▪ Extend patterning experiences to other activities in your program. Point out incidental patterns children create as they work with materials such as pegs, beads, and Lego pieces. Take walks to look for patterns inside and outdoors.

▪ Older fours may enjoy making patterns for each other to copy. Photographs of child-made patterns can be displayed where children can refer to them as they play.

BOOKS

| Here are some good books for observing patterns around us. | ▪ *Zoo City* by Stephen Lewis (Greenwillow Books) | ▪ *Changes, Changes* by Pat Hutchins (Macmillan) | ▪ *Look Again* by Tana Hoban (Macmillan) |

BLOCKS

Imaginations will soar as your children combine these blocks and props to create miniature environments.

THE MINIATURE WORLD OF BLOCKS

Aim: Children will use their imaginations and creative-thinking skills as they combine blocks and accessories to create miniature environments.

Group Size: Three to four children.

Materials: Small unit or table blocks; art materials such as cotton balls, construction paper, aluminum foil, play-dough, cloth and wallpaper scraps, and floor tiles; shoe-boxes; and small accessories such as dolls, plastic animals, dinosaurs, trees, small vehicles, trains and train tracks, bottle caps, empty thread spools, etc. (Make sure items pass a choke tube test.)

GETTING READY

Gather a small group of children and show them some of the accessories such as the little dolls, animals, and dinosaurs. Have children look at the items, and talk about how they have used them with blocks. Then introduce the cotton balls, shoe box, thread spools, and others, and ask, "How could you use these with the other toys?"

Then say, "Close your eyes really, really tight and think of some make-believe worlds you could make with these toys in the block area." Then have children open their eyes and share their ideas.

BEGIN

Have children move to the block area and start to collect the items they need. Allow children time to begin their creations, and offer assistance when needed. As children work, see if there are additional materials they need.

After a while, ask questions or make comments to clarify children's ideas and dramas such as, "It looks like you've turned the shoe box into a cave. Do those dinosaurs live there? How do they get in and out?" Or, "I see you have built a place with lots of little rooms. Who will live in all of these rooms?"

Offer the art materials after the children have completed the building phase of the project. Fabric and wallpaper scraps can be taped to buildings to form walls, curtains, or enclosures. Invite children to create additional uses for these and others.

Remember

▪ This project could take place over many days so that children can slowly add to and play with their creations. You may want to create a special area for building so that the constructions can stay up for a few days.

▪ Children will enjoy creating stories about their worlds. Some may wish to dictate their stories and add illustrations. Display these with photographs of their work, and later turn them into a "big book" to add to your library.

BOOKS

| Here are some picture books for inspiration. | ▪ *Airport* by Byron Barton (Crowell) | ▪ *The City* by Douglas Florian (Crowell) | ▪ *Big Red Barn* by Margaret Wise Brown (Addison-Wesley) |

BLOCKS

Even though children use the same blocks, their buildings are always different!

SAME BLOCKS, DIFFERENT BUILDINGS

Aim: Your children will use observation, comparison, and perceptual skills as they compare their constructions to a friend's.

Group Size: Two children at a time.

Materials: Matching sets of unit blocks or table blocks of various sizes and shapes, and cardboard blocks or a low divider.

GETTING READY

Discuss the concepts of "same" and "different." Use classroom objects to demonstrate the concepts. Play a matching game where children match objects that are the same. For instance, ask, "What makes this crayon the same as the other one? Now what makes this one different?" Then invite children to join you in the block area for a matching activity.

BEGIN

Move to the block area and ask children to help you assemble two sets of blocks that are the same. This is a good matching activity that helps them understand the concept of "same." As children find the matching blocks, have them sort the blocks into separate piles.

Before the children begin, have them build a wall between them using the large hollow or cardboard blocks. (You can also use a low divider or screen.)

Now explain to the children that they are to begin. Remind them that both sets of blocks are the same. Then ask, "Do you think your buildings will look alike? Let's see what happens. The trick to this game is that you won't be able to see what your friend is building!"

Encourage children to build with the blocks any way they wish. When they are both finished, remove the wall or divider so they can see each other's buildings. Ask, "How is your building different from your friend's? Are there things that are the same about them?" Have children walk around the buildings to examine all sides. Which is the longest? The highest?

Remember

▪ Children may not be able to see the differences in their structures right away. You may need to help them verbalize the differences by pointing out a few at first.

BOOKS

Enjoy these books about differences.

▪ *Becca Backward, Becca Frontward* by Bruce McMillan (Lothrop, Lee & Shepard)

▪ *Super, Super, Superwords* by Bruce McMillan (Lothrop, Lee & Shepard)

▪ *Bigger and Smaller* by Robert Froman (Thomas Y. Crowell)

BLOCKS

The circus is in town and on its way to your block corner!

UNDER THE BIG TOP!

Aim: Children will use problem-solving, dramatic-play, fine-motor, and creative-thinking skills as they create a circus.

Group Size: Three to four children at a time.

Materials: Unit or table blocks; three Hula-Hoops or similar large hoops; toy animals and people; an old clean sheet or blanket; tape and string; markers; circus books and pictures; and balloons.

GETTING READY

This is a great activity to try when the circus is in town. Encourage those children who have been to the circus to

share their experiences with the group. Ask, "What was it like? What did you see? What did you like the best? What animals did you see?" Then read one of the books below.

Ask, "What if we made our own circus using blocks? What should we include?" Have children brainstorm a list of things to include in your circus. Record them on a rebus chart, and hang it in the block area as a reminder. Hang any circus pictures or posters you have in the block area as well.

BEGIN

Explain that a circus often has three rings, and that each ring features a different circus act. Ask your children to decide on how many rings they want their circus to have. Then ask, "What could we use to make the rings?" Have children share their ideas. Later, show children the blanket or sheet. Say, "Maybe we could use this as our 'big top.'" Have children think of different ways to stack tall towers of blocks to hold the big top. (Large cardboard blocks would work well, and the fabric could be draped over.)

Now encourage the children to work on their own, using the blocks and accessories to create circus acts, seats for the audience, homes for the animals, platforms for performances, and other ideas they may have suggested.

As they work, offer new ideas and additional accessories. For instance, "Here are some string and tape. Maybe you could use these for the tightrope and trapeze."

Encourage children to fill up the rings with animals performing different acts in each ring. Help them attach "performing" trapeze and tightrope artists to the string with tape.

Then put on some music and let the circus begin. Invite other children in your group to come see what's happening under the big top!

Remember

- Younger fours may lack the skills and patience to make complex structures and props. They may prefer to build something quickly and spend the rest of the time playing out circus activities.
- Extend this idea to dramatic-play activities. Children can create a circus using large blocks where they can be the performing animals and people.
- Older children might be ready for cooperative ventures and a long term project ending with a performance.

BOOKS

| Here are some books to share about the circus. | ▪ *Circus* by Mattie Lou O'Kelly (Little, Brown) | ▪ *Circus Baby* by Maud Petersham (Macmillan) | ▪ *Bearymore* by Don Freeman (Viking Penguin) |

BLOCKS

Your experienced block builders may enjoy building around these obstacles.

OVER, UNDER, AROUND, AND THROUGH

Aim: Children will use problem-solving skills as they build around different obstacles with blocks.
Group Size: Three or four children.
Materials: Unit blocks, a large cardboard carton with the top and bottom cut off, a small table, a chair, a low room divider, and a few large cardboard blocks.

IN ADVANCE

Place these "obstacles" in the block area, spacing them apart so that children have room to build around them, over them, through them, and under them.

GETTING READY

Ask children if they have ever been on an obstacle course. Set up a mini-course using some objects in your room. Then explain that to get through the course there are objects in your path that you have to go over, under, around, and through. Have children practice going through this mini-course.

Now lead children to the block area. Say, "Here are some obstacles to build around. How can we use blocks to build over, under, around, and through these obstacles?" Allow children some time to think and share their ideas about each question.

BEGIN

Have the children closely examine the obstacles. Then ask, "Which ones can you build through? Which ones can you build over?" Encourage children to share their ideas with everyone, and to think of ways to incorporate obstacles into their constructions.

Allow children ample time to experiment with ways to build with or around the obstacles. Later, comment on your observations: "I see you are building under the table. Can you also build around it?" Or, "Your block construction goes right through this box. It starts on this side and comes out on the other side." Help individual children as needed.

After children are done, give them time to talk about their constructions. Encourage them to describe how they used the obstacles in their constructions using the words *over*, *under*,

around, and *through*.

Remember

▪ Experienced builders will enjoy the challenge of this activity. Follow-up discussions might focus on which were easier or harder to build and why. This is a good time to talk about problem-solving strategies including what worked, what didn't, and ideas they might use in the future.
▪ To simplify this activity for less experienced builders, use only one concept each day, beginning with the easiest to build. For example, set up several objects under which children could build. Encourage children to help each other, and offer your assistance if needed.
▪ Another day, you can have children build an obstacle course out of blocks that they can go through.

BOOKS

| Here are some books to share after the activity. | ▪ *Where Is My Friend?* by Betsy Maestro (Crown) | ▪ *Over, Under & Through* by Tana Hoban (Macmillan) | ▪ *We're Going on a Bear Hunt* by Michael Rosen (McElderry) |

BLOCKS

Here are some ways for your four-year-olds to experiment with balance.

BALANCE IT!

Aim: Children will use observation, comparison, and prediction skills while weighing blocks on a pan balance scale.
Group Size: Four to five children.
Materials: Unit, table, or color cube blocks; a pan balance scale; newsprint paper; and markers.

GETTING READY

Allow children time to play in the block area alone for a while. Then casually go over and give a few children the pan balance scale. Say, "Here is something you might like to use with the blocks today. I'll come back to pick it up later."

Observe what children do with the scale. Do they load blocks on one pan? What do they do when the other pan tips up? Do they place blocks on both sides?

BEGIN

After a while, go back over and say, "I noticed you were using the balance scale. How does it work? What did you try?" Allow children time to share their experiences with the scale.

Then explain that it's a pan balance scale and can be used to weigh things. Have a child put a large block on one of the pans. Now point out how one pan is up and the other is down. Explain that the pan with the block weighs more, and that's why it went down. Then say, "I wonder if there's something we can put on the other pan to make them even?" Give children time to respond. If needed, suggest that maybe another block might help. Have children select a block or blocks to try.

When the scale balances, point out the position of the pans, and explain that now they weigh the same.

Now allow the children to experiment with placing different blocks on the pans. Invite them to guess how many small blocks are needed to balance one big block. Allow children ample time to make predictions, and then test them.

Later, children will enjoy going around the classroom to pick out objects to weigh with blocks. Have them collect small toys, dolls, and animals. Let them guess which items will "weigh the most blocks," then test out their predictions.

Remember

▪ The balance scale will be new to many children. Allow children plenty of time to experiment with it before and after the activity.
▪ Experiment with balance using blocks alone. For example, have children try to balance different-shaped blocks on the point of a triangle block, on a standing square or rectangle, or on a curved block. Talk about why some are more difficult than others.

BOOKS

Here are some books to share after this activity.

▪ *Balance It* by Howard Smith (Four Winds)

▪ *All Shapes and Sizes* by Shirley Hughes (Lothrop, Lee & Shepard)

▪ *The Way Things Work* by David Macaulay (Houghton Mifflin)

BLOCKS

Challenge your children's building and problem-solving skills with these ideas!

TASK CARD BUILDINGS

Aim: Children use creative-thinking skills as they build constructions with a limited number of blocks.

Group Size: Three or four children.

Materials: Wooden unit blocks of various sizes and shapes; construction paper or poster board; and markers.

IN ADVANCE

Cut 8-10 large squares out of construction paper or poster board. Select a variety of unit blocks and draw (or trace) one block outline on each paper square. (There should be one outline per card.) Include unit blocks, cylinders, triangles, curves, pillars, etc. Select blocks of which you have a large number.

Later children will pull 2-3 cards at random, and then use the blocks indicated to build a construction.

GETTING READY

Gather a few children in the block area. Ask, "What would it be like if you only had triangle and cylinder blocks to build with? Or just squares and curves? What could you build?" Allow children time to respond.

Show them the cards with the outlines. How many outlines do they recognize? Can they find the matching blocks?

Turn the cards face down, and allow each child to select 2-3 cards. Tell them that these will be the blocks they will use to build and play. Once the children have selected their cards, have them gather the matching blocks.

BEGIN

Give children time to start their constructions. Observe them to see how their constructions are coming along. Aside from building with the blocks, encourage children to create designs or patterns with the blocks, too. How many different designs can they come up with? How many different patterns? You can also challenge them by saying, "Can you build a house with the blocks you have? A boat? A bridge?"

After children have had time to work alone, suggest that they join up with a friend and "pool" their shapes to create something together. Ask, "Is it harder or easier to use only two kinds of blocks? Why or why not?"

You can also let children trade in their cards and select new cards with which to build.

Remember

▪ Young fours may find this activity too limiting. Introduce cards only after children have had lots of block-building experience using ideas of their own.

▪ Take a trip to look at buildings made of brick. Look closely to see how they are constructed. Are the bricks all the same size and shape? If some are different from most, where are they used? Ask children why they think those bricks were used there and to guess what might happen if different shapes were used.

BOOKS

Try these books after children have finished building.	▪ *Demi's Opposites* by Demi (Grosset & Dunlap)	▪ *Mr. Bear's Chair* by Thomas Graham (Dutton)	▪ *Mr. Bear's Boat* by Thomas Graham (Dutton)

BLOCKS

Make trails and roads out of unit blocks. Then have fun knocking them down!

BUILDING BLOCK "DOMINO" TRAILS

Aim: Children will use problem-solving, fine-motor, estimating, and predicting skills as they create various types of block "domino" trails.
Group Size: Three or four children.
Materials: Unit blocks, masking tape, paper, and markers.

GETTING READY

Building domino block trails and knocking them down is always a big hit. (For some children it may be a new experience.) First, show children how to carefully stand blocks on end in a row. Use this to demonstrate why the blocks need to be close together. Line up three or four blocks close to each other. Then line up the same number of blocks spaced farther apart. Invite children to gently push over the first block of each trail. Ask, "Which trail kept falling? Why?"

Give children plenty of time to experiment with this trail-building technique. Encourage them to try blocks of different shapes and sizes and trails of different lengths.

BEGIN

Put masking tape on the floor to use as outlines for trails. Start off with simple straight lines. Then try some with wide, gentle curves. (Hard angles are too difficult for young children to handle.) Suggest that children line up the blocks on the trails and then gently knock them down. Did they set up enough blocks to complete the trail? As children's abilities improve, help them create trails that are more difficult.

Ready, Set...GO!

Try having a race! Ask, "Which line will take longer to knock down, a straight line or a curved line?" Use masking tape again to create one of each on the floor. Then suggest that children line up the blocks. When the blocks have been set up, have children predict which trail they think will win. Record their predictions on a chart or graph. Then have a countdown to start the race!

Try this many times with different trails, and record children's predictions.

Remember

▪ You may wish to draw trails rather than use tape on the floor. Tape large sheets of newsprint together, or use rolls of craft, shelf, or butcher paper. Children will enjoy drawing trails, and favorite ones can be saved to use over and over.
▪ This is a good activity to integrate math skills for older fives. Children can measure lengths of trails and space between blocks using a variety of measures (for example, counting cubes, Unifix or Cuisenaire Rods, or rulers). Graphs can record numbers of blocks used and/or lengths of trails.

BOOKS			
Here are a few related books to add to the fun.	▪ *Changes, Changes* by Pat Hutchins (Macmillan)	▪ *Have You Seen Roads?* by Joanne Oppenheim (Random House)	▪ *Rain, Rain, Rivers* by Uri Schulevitz (Charles Scribner's Sons)

BLOCKS

Help your children create a little corner of their neighborhood in the block area.

NEIGHBORHOOD MAPS

Aim: Children will use creative-thinking, problem-solving, and spatial-awareness skills as they cooperate in the construction of a neighborhood map.

Group Size: Four to six children

Materials: Unit or table blocks; masking or colored tape; construction paper; junk-type materials such as egg cartons, tubes, small boxes and containers; experience-chart paper; markers; and a local map (optional).

GETTING READY

Walk together around the neighborhood. Look carefully at the buildings closest to your preschool or center. Point out important roads and buildings nearby. When you come back inside, record children's observations on an experience chart.

BEGIN

Talk about maps and, if possible, locate where your street or building is on a local map. Then explain that you're going to make your own neighborhood "map" out of blocks.

Provide construction paper and tape and help children construct a "floor" for your map. Use tape to make the roads, green paper for yards and parks, etc. Next talk about what buildings to include. (It's best to start with your center, and then move to buildings further away.)

Use the blocks and junk-type accessories to create the structures.

Improving the Neighborhood

When the children have finished the map, ask them to consider ways they would like to change the neighborhood and make it better. Ask, "What would you like to add to your neighborhood? What would make it more fun?" Encourage children to use their imaginations. They may come up with everything from a giant swimming pool to a pony in every backyard!

Before making the improvements on the "old" neighborhood, take a few pictures of it. After the changes have been made, take some photographs of the "new and improved" neighborhood.

Later, have children dictate a story about the experience and display the photos.

Remember

▪ If possible, take photographs of the buildings and significant landmarks you see on your walk. Add these to the experience chart, and have children refer to them as they work.

▪ Young fives may need to do some simple block mapping activities before beginning this project. Suggest making floor plan "maps" showing the furniture arrangement of a familiar room at home or in your program environment. As skills increase, graduate to maps of several rooms, the buildings on just your street, the activity areas and equipment of a play yard or playground, etc.

▪ Keep in mind that accuracy is not the most important aspect of this project. The process children work through is key. They learn from the experience of interpreting real life into block forms.

BOOKS

Here are some good books about neighborhoods.	▪ *All Kinds of Signs* by Seymour Reit (Western)	▪ *The House With the Red Roof* by William Wise (Putnam Publishing Group)	▪ *The Little House* by Virginia Burton (Houghton Mifflin)

BLOCKS

Make way for these new homes on the block!

HOME SWEET HOME

Aim: Children will use problem-solving and creative-thinking skills as they construct different homes out of blocks.
Group Size: Three to four children.
Materials: Unit and cardboard blocks; pictures of homes and apartment buildings from magazines and books; experience-chart paper and markers; and accessories such as carpet squares, floor tiles, fabric remnants, curtains, artificial plants and flowers, doll furniture, and small dolls.

IN ADVANCE

On cardboard, mount magazine pictures of homes such as log cabins, bungalows, farmhouses, apartment buildings, suburban homes, brownstones, trailers, hotels, and houseboats. If possible, include the homes of some of your children. (Ask parents to send in photos.)

GETTING READY

Discuss the different types of homes in which people live. Let your children take turns talking about their homes. How many live in apartment buildings? Shelters? Private homes? Trailers? Hotels? Then have children brainstorm the different types of homes they have seen in the community. Take a walk around the neighborhood to look at the homes and dwellings people live in nearby.

Point out the different materials that the homes are made out of such as wood, bricks, stones, etc. Look for windows, doors, porches, roofs, chimneys, awnings, and outdoor stoops or steps leading to apartment buildings. Look above storefronts for apartments and point them out.

When you come back to your center, have children create an experience chart about the homes they saw.

BEGIN

Ask the children if they would like to try to build some homes in the block area. Put up some of the pictures of homes. Encourage children to work cooperatively to build them. Remind them of the homes they saw on the walk, and encourage them to try different types. Will their homes have an upstairs and downstairs? What about apartments? Will

they be located above a store or in their own buildings? How many floors will they have? Will their homes be in the country near a field or in the city near a park? Children also may want to re-create their own homes in blocks.

Help children collect the materials they need, and be available to offer assistance and guidance.

After children have completed their homes, give them an opportunity to talk about them. Have them invite friends from their class and others to come see the new homes on the block!

Remember

• Children may want to make complex structures that are beyond their abilities. Be prepared to help them scale down

grandiose ideas to more manageable ones. Let them try some challenging ideas. Offer help with planning and problem-solving. If children insist on more difficult ideas, consider making it a cooperative and long-term project.
• After this experience with blocks, children might be interested in making permanent structures. Use sturdy cardboard boxes or wooden crates turned on their sides for an open "dollhouse" view of the inside. Partition them into rooms with cardboard, then furnish and decorate.

BOOKS

Here are some good books about houses.	• *A House for Everyone* by Betty Miles (Random House)	• *The Little Stone House* by Berta and Elmer Hader (Macmillan)	• *Tony's Hard Work Day* by Alan Arkin (Harper & Row)

BLOCKS

Your children will see how they "stack up" by measuring each other with blocks.

HOW MANY BLOCKS TALL AM I?

Aim: Children will use observation and problem-solving skills as they measure themselves with blocks.
Group Size: Four children at a time.
Materials: Unit blocks, a large sheet of paper, rulers, and a tape measure.

GETTING READY

Invite a few children to join you, and show them the yard-stick or tape measure. Do any of them recognize these measuring tools? If so, who has seen someone use them? What were they measuring? Then demonstrate how they are used by measuring different things in the classroom.

Ask children if they can remember the last time they had their heights measured. At the doctor's office perhaps? Do they remember what the doctor used? Then say, "I bet it might be fun to measure ourselves with blocks. I wonder how tall each of us would be with blocks. Let's go to the block area to see."

BEGIN

Decide on which unit blocks you'll use for measurement.

The unit or half-unit blocks would be good ones to use.

Suggest that children work in pairs to measure each other. The child being measured stands straight and tall. The child's partner builds a tower next to him or her, and stops when the tower is equal to the child's height. Then together, they count how many blocks are in the stack. That will tell them how tall the child is in unit blocks! Then they trade places and the other child is measured.

After everyone has had a turn, children can record their block measurements on an experience chart.

Remember

- After children have had some experience with this, play a game where they guess how tall someone is in blocks. After they are measured, whose guess comes closest?
- Encourage children to measure other things in the room such as shelves, table heights, chairs, etc.
- If it is too hard to build towers as tall as children, have children lie on the floor, and place blocks end-to-end alongside them.

BOOKS
Share these books to enhance children's experiences.

- *Super, Super, Superwords* by Bruce McMillan (Lothrop, Lee & Shepard)
- *Is It Larger, Is It Smaller?* by Tana Hoban (Greenwillow)
- *What's That Size?* by Kate Petty (Franklin Watts)

BLOCKS

How far and how fast will balls and cars roll off the ramps your children build?

EXPERIMENTING WITH BLOCKS AND BOARDS

Aim: Children use problem-solving and reasoning skills and cause and effect as they experiment with constructing ramps.
Group Size: Three to four children.
Materials: Two boards of equal length (to use as ramps), hollow cardboard blocks, unit blocks, vehicles, and small rubber balls.

IN ADVANCE

Set up a ramp in the block area using a board. Place a hollow block or stack of unit blocks under one end of the board, lifting it about 12 inches off the floor. Park cars and trucks nearby.

BEGIN

When children arrive in the block area, tell them you have something set up for them to experiment with on their own. Show them the balls, cars, and trucks and tell them that you'll return later.

Observe to see how children use the materials. Do they roll the balls and cars down the ramp? Do the cars roll smoothly or fall off the side? Do the children add walls or blocks to the sides or at the bottom of the ramp?

Go back after a while and say, "I wonder what will happen if you make the ramp higher? Lower?" Or, "I noticed that the cars seem to fall off the ramp. I wonder how you could stop that from happening? Do you think a wall along the ramp would help?"

Children can also build tunnels out of curved blocks, or add parking lots and garages at the end of the ramps to add more purpose to their play.

Observe children's continued efforts and offer guidance when needed.

Best Guesses

Once they have had lots of time to experiment on their own, say, "Let's have a race." Have children use the other board to make a second ramp. Have them build this ramp

next to the first one and make it a little higher. Then ask, "Which ramp do you think will make the cars run faster?" Have each child make a guess. Then set the cars up on the ramps and let them go! Ask the children to tell why they think the higher ramp was faster.

Have children adjust the heights of the ramps again. Now ask them to guess how far they think the balls will roll. Have them mark the spot on the floor with tape. Then ask, "Which ramp will make the ball roll farther away?" Then have children test their predictions.

For added fun and challenge, children can set up small figures, toys, or empty boxes at the end of the ramps to knock down. How high or low will the ramps have to be to reach the targets?

Remember

▪ You may want to introduce different aspects of ramp play over a few days. This way children can have more time to experiment with ideas and understand the cause and effect of their actions.
▪ Offer your older fives string or yarn to measure the distance their cars or balls travel as they come off the ramp. If marking the floor with tape is impractical, set up ramps on long sheets of paper, and use crayons to mark the spots.

BOOKS

Here are some books that will inspire more ramp building.	▪ *New Road* by Gail Gibbons (Thomas Y. Crowell)	▪ *Changes, Changes* by Pat Hutchins (Macmillan)	▪ *If You Look Around You* by Fulvio Testa (Dial Books)

BLOCKS

The sky's the limit when your children take block building outdoors!

BUILDING OUTDOORS

Aim: Children use gross-motor and creative-thinking skills as they build with blocks on the playground.

Group Size: Four children at a time.

Materials: Cardboard or wooden boxes; planks and boards; an old sheet or blanket; hollow wooden blocks or cardboard blocks; and a wagon and riding toys.

IN ADVANCE

Just before you leave to go outdoors, tell the children that there will be some new materials on the playground for them

to play with. Show them the items and ask, "How do you think you could use these on the playground? What could you build?" Encourage children to share their ideas.

Then have children help carry some of these objects outdoors. They can use wagons to cart the blocks. Or the boxes can be filled with blocks and carried outside by an adult.

GETTING READY

Select an area on the playground away from high traffic areas to set up the blocks, boards, and boxes. Allow children to come over on their own since outdoor play should be a time for children to pursue their own play interests.

BEGIN

As children come over to investigate the building materials, observe to see if they have some ideas of their own. If not, you can make a few suggestions and then leave them on their own to play.

Some possible ideas may be for children to create a large outdoor tent or cave that can serve as the "safe" areas during chase games, or as a place to hide away.

You can also suggest that children take advantage of the space and create long bridges to drive their trikes under. Gas stations and car washes can be built for trikes to get a wash and gas. Finally, using the boxes and blocks, children can create oversized vehicles like long trains, buses, or planes.

Suggest these ideas, and assist children when needed — only if they seem to need an idea to get started. But they will undoubtedly have many ideas of their own!

Remember

- Leave plenty of time for cleanup and transporting materials back inside. Supply rags or paper towels to wipe off blocks.
- Take safety precautions — check wooden boxes and boards for rough edges; help children find level ground to build on; limit the height of structures; make sure buildings are steady before permitting children to use them; and, if needed, limit the number of children playing at a time.

BOOKS

Here are some books to share when you come back indoors.

- *For Rent* by Charles E. Martin (Greenwell)

- *The Little House* by Virginia Lee Burton (Houghton Mifflin)

- *Machines as Tall as Giants* by Paul Stickland (Random)

BLOCKS

Here's a cooperative block game that your experienced builders will enjoy.

TRADING PLACES

Aim: Children will use problem-solving and decision-making skills as they complete each other's constructions.
Group Size: Two to four children at a time.
Materials: Unit blocks and a timer.

GETTING READY

After children have had ample time to play with blocks on their own, ask a few children if they would like to play a game. Gather the interested children together and show them the timer. Show them how it works so they are familiar with the sound of the timer when it goes off.

Tell the children that the activity involves selecting a partner and then building something with him or her. The timer is used to let them know when to start and stop building.

BEGIN

Have children select a building partner. Have each child collect a pile of blocks and sit back to back. Suggest that each child think of an idea of something to build — or tell them to create something as they go along. Then ask the children to let you know when they are ready.

Turn on the timer, and observe quietly as the children build. At the end of the three minutes have the children stop. Give them time to collect more blocks, if needed. Then have them trade places.

Turn on the timer, and have the children make additions to each other's buildings for three more minutes. When the timer goes off, have the children stop and look at their constructions.

How have the constructions changed? Are they taller? Wider? What new blocks were added? Encourage children to describe what they added to each other's constructions. Help them by pointing out the differences you notice.

Have each child tell what his or her building started out to be. Then ask each building partner to tell what it became!

Another time have children decide in advance what each building will be. Then as partners, they will take turns building them.

Remember

▪ Try not to make this a competitive activity. The children work together as partners, not as competitors.
▪ If a Polaroid camera is available, have children take photographs of their buildings before they trade places. The photo will help them note the differences more easily.

BOOKS

Try these books at storytime.

▪ *Changes, Changes* by Pat Hutchins (Macmillan)

▪ *The Story of a Main Street* by John S. Goodal (Macmillan)

▪ *A Regular Rolling Noah* by George E. Lyon (Bradbury)

BLOCKS

Children are fascinated with dinosaurs and will feel powerful creating an island for these huge animals!

DINOSAUR ISLAND

Aim: Children will use creative-thinking skills as they cooperate to build a play environment.

Group Size: Three to four children.

Materials: Unit, cardboard, and table blocks; an assortment of plastic and toy dinosaurs; clay or playdough; leaves or plastic plants; Popsicle sticks; shoeboxes; construction paper; and pictures of dinosaurs.

GETTING READY

Children are naturally intrigued by dinosaurs and other prehistoric animals. Gather some pictures and bring together a small group of interested children. Show children the pictures, and have them share their knowledge of dinosaurs with you. Talk about the size of the dinosaurs. Then have children think of the largest animals they can — like elephants or giraffes — and explain that many prehistoric animals were larger than all of them!

Look at the pictures to see what the world looked like when dinosaurs lived. Were there houses, cars, or stores? Then point out the trees and plants, the mountains, the oceans, the caves, and the rocks and cliffs to the children.

Ask children if they would like to build an island of dinosaurs in the block area!

BEGIN

Have children begin by creating a base out of blocks for the island. Explain that an island is land that is surrounded by water on all sides. Show pictures if you have them. Then ask, "How do you think we could build the island. Which blocks would work best?" (The island is really a platform of blocks on which children may build the trees and other land areas. The floor space surrounding the "island" could be the ocean.)

After the base has been constructed, allow children to work on their own to build the mountains, trees, caves, and other land forms. As they work, provide additional props and accessories to spark new ideas. Trees can be built by sticking Popsicle sticks into clay and adding paper or playdough for leaves. Children can make additional dinosaurs from playdough. Cardboard blocks make tall mountains, and blue mural paper can surround the island as water for dinosaurs to swim in.

Allow this project to take place over a few days so that children can create and expand on a variety of dramatic-play themes and ideas. Have them create stories about the "happenings" on Dinosaur Island and make a book about them!

Remember

- Display pictures of dinosaurs, mountains, trees, and caves on the wall in the block area for inspiration.
- Extend this activity by offering children opportunities to make their own individual dinosaur habitats to take home. Dioramas and other miniature habitats can be made using materials such as clay, wood scraps, cardboard, and paper. Set up an area where these can be displayed museum style, and have children create signs and stories for the exhibit. Invite other classes and parents to visit the "Dinosaur Museum."

BOOKS

| Inspire children with these stories before they begin! | • *How I Captured a Dinosaur* by Henry Schwartz (Orchard Books) | • *Tyrone the Horrible* by Hans Wilhelm (Scholastic) | • *Patrick's Dinosaurs* by Carol Carrick (Clarion) |

BLOCKS

Now your fives can build the rooms of their dreams — with blocks!

A ROOM JUST FOR ME!

Aim: This activity enhances children's self-esteem as they create their ideal rooms, and then have an opportunity to talk about them.

Group Size: Two or three children.

Materials: Unit blocks, cardboard and hollow blocks; planks and boards; boxes; assorted props like pillows, floor tiles, blankets, rug remnants, and wallpaper samples; sleeping bags; construction paper; and a Polaroid camera and film (optional).

GETTING READY

During circle time ask children to describe what their "perfect" room would be. Where would it be? What would it look like? What kind of furniture and toys would they have? Would they have a bed, a bunk bed, or sleep in a sleeping bag? Would they have a TV?

Then invite children to build a room or home of their own with blocks.

BEGIN

Show children some of the props and encourage them to think of what their room would look like. How tall will it be? How wide? Will it have a door? Then allow them to select the blocks they need to get started.

Allow children to construct on their own for a while. Then comment from time to time on your observations, and offer assistance when needed. Encourage them to use the blocks and boxes to build furniture and other things they want for their rooms. Then introduce new props as their constructions near completion. Encourage the children to draw pictures and posters to hang on the walls of their room. They can also construct appliances or other props in the woodworking area to add to their rooms.

When the children's rooms are done, bring the other children in your group together, and allow the builders to talk about the rooms and furnishings. Ask the builders questions about their rooms, and encourage the other children to do so as well.

Later, take pictures of the children's rooms, and record their descriptions to display.

Remember
▪ Young fives may prefer to create child-size rooms and furnishings to use for dramatic play.
▪ Older fives can make miniature rooms with unit or table blocks along with dollhouse-size furniture and people. Later they may wish to use art and woodworking materials to construct permanent rooms.

BOOKS

| Here are some books to share with children in their special "rooms." | ▪ *The Lost and Found House* by Consuelo Joerns (Four Winds) | ▪ *A Chair for My Mother* by Vera B. Williams (Greenwillow) | ▪ *Block City* by Robert Louis Stevenson (Dutton) |

BLOCKS

Pack your bags, and join your fives as they take off to build new worlds!

WE'RE ON THE MOON!

Aim: Children will engage in dramatic play as they use creative-thinking and problem-solving skills to create the surface of the moon.

Group Size: Three to four children.

Materials: Unit and cardboard blocks; an old sheet; an appliance box or other large box; aluminum foil; mural paper; flashlights; large pillows; and assorted junk materials.

GETTING READY

Read one of the books below, or another story about space travel. Follow the story up with some pictures of the moon or other planets. Then ask, "Would you ever want to travel to outer space? Would you ever go to the moon?" Encourage children to respond. Have them tell what they think it looks like, what they would take with them, etc.

Then ask, "How do you think we could use blocks to create the moon? What other things would we need?"

Invite children to try out their ideas in the block area.

BEGIN

Have children look at pictures of the moon. Point out the stars around the moon, the bumpy surface, the craters, etc. Then say, "Since no one lives on the moon yet, there are no houses. We could be the first people to build houses on the moon! I wonder what they would look like?"

Then look over the available props and materials, and discuss how they might be used to create the moon's surface and homes. The sheet could represent the surface of the moon. Cardboard blocks under the sheet could create large craters. Boxes could be used as bases for the moon homes or moon vehicles. Blocks and boxes can be covered in foil to represent metal. Foil also makes great stars. Allow children to work on their own. Offer guidance and suggestions when needed, and observe quietly from time to time.

Later, come back and make comments based on your observations. Have children talk about the moon homes and vehicles. Have them tell how they created and built different parts of the moon itself.

Since it's so dark around the moon, ask children if they would like to turn out the lights and use flashlights to see how their moon looks. Look for interesting shadows and stars. Allow children to play "on the moon" in the darkened room with the flashlights to inspire new play themes and ideas.

Remember

▪ After children finish building, suggest they add miniature people and other small props, and provide plenty of time for them to play with their moonscapes.

BOOKS

Here are some books to share before and after the moon journey.

▪ *Happy Birthday Moon* by Frank Asch (Simon & Schuster)

▪ *Papa Please Get the Moon for Me* by Eric Carle (Picture Book Studio)

▪ *Regards to the Man in the Moon* by Ezra Jack Keats (Four Winds)

ACTIVITY PLAN INDEX:
TWOS AND THREES

DEVELOPMENTAL AREAS AND SKILLS ENHANCED	GROSS-MOTOR	FINE-MOTOR	CAUSE/EFFECT	EXPRESSIVE LANGUAGE	COOPERATION/ SOCIAL INTERACT.	SORTING/ CLASSIFYING	OBSERVING	PROBLEM-SOLVING	DRAMATIC PLAY	MAKING COMPARISONS	CREATIVE THINKING	EYE/HAND COORDINATION
2'S ACTIVITY PLANS												
PAINT THE BLOCKS: WASH THEM CLEAN! PAGE 38	■	■	■		■		■	■				■
FEELY BAG BLOCKS PAGE 39		■		■	■	■	■			■		
"MAKE AND PLAY" BOX BLOCKS PAGE 40	■	■		■	■			■			■	■
TUMBLING TOWERS PAGE 41	■	■	■			■	■	■				■
HOW HIGH? PAGE 42	■	■		■	■		■			■		■
BUSY, BUSY ROADS PAGE 43	■	■		■						■		
THEY ALL FALL DOWN PAGE 44	■	■	■		■			■			■	
BLOCK SHAPE SORTERS PAGE 45		■				■	■	■				■
TOTE THOSE BLOCKS PAGE 46	■	■			■				■			
YOU ADD ONE, AND I'LL ADD ONE PAGE 47		■		■	■		■				■	■
3'S ACTIVITY PLANS												
LET'S GO BLOCK BOWLING PAGE 48	■		■	■	■				■			■
MUSICAL BLOCKS PAGE 49	■	■			■			■				
APPLIANCE BOX STRUCTURES PAGE 50	■			■	■			■	■		■	
LET'S BUILD A ZOO PAGE 51		■		■	■			■	■			
BLOCKS IN THE SANDBOX PAGE 52	■	■	■	■	■		■				■	■
FOLLOW THE LEADER WITH BLOCKS! PAGE 53		■		■	■		■			■		■
MY HIDEAWAY PAGE 54	■	■			■			■	■		■	
SHINING SILVER SKYSCRAPERS PAGE 55		■	■	■			■				■	■
CREATING SOFT SPOTS WITH BLOCKS PAGE 56				■	■				■	■	■	
CASTING SHADOWS IN THE GREAT OUTDOORS PAGE 57	■	■	■	■	■		■			■	■	

ACTIVITY PLAN INDEX: FOURS AND FIVES

DEVELOPMENTAL AREAS AND SKILLS ENHANCED	GROSS-MOTOR	FINE-MOTOR	CAUSE/EFFECT	EXPRESSIVE LANGUAGE	COOPERATION/SOCIAL INTERACT.	SORTING/CLASSIFYING	OBSERVING	PROBLEM-SOLVING	DRAMATIC PLAY	MAKING COMPARISONS	CREATIVE THINKING	EYE/HAND COORDINATION
4'S ACTIVITY PLANS												
MAKING BLOCK FURNITURE PAGE 58	■	■		■	■			■	■		■	■
MAZES AND BALLS PAGE 59		■			■	■	■	■			■	■
"STARTER" BUILDINGS PAGE 60		■					■	■		■	■	■
PATTERNING WITH BLOCKS PAGE 61		■		■			■	■		■	■	
THE MINIATURE WORLD OF BLOCKS PAGE 62		■		■				■	■		■	
SAME BLOCKS, DIFFERENT BUILDINGS PAGE 63		■		■		■	■	■		■		
UNDER THE BIG TOP! PAGE 64		■		■	■			■	■		■	
OVER, UNDER, AROUND, AND THROUGH PAGE 65	■	■					■	■			■	■
BALANCE IT! PAGE 66		■	■	■			■	■		■		■
TASK CARD BUILDINGS PAGE 67	■	■						■		■	■	■
5'S ACTIVITY PLANS												
BUILDING BLOCK "DOMINO" TRAILS PAGE 68		■	■				■	■		■		■
NEIGHBORHOOD MAPS PAGE 69	■			■	■		■		■		■	
HOME SWEET HOME PAGE 70		■			■			■	■		■	
HOW MANY BLOCKS TALL AM I? PAGE 71		■			■		■	■		■		■
EXPERIMENTING WITH BLOCKS AND BOARDS PAGE 72	■	■	■		■		■	■			■	■
BUILDING OUTDOORS PAGE 73	■	■			■			■	■		■	
TRADING PLACES PAGE 74		■		■	■		■	■			■	
DINOSAUR ISLAND PAGE 75	■	■		■	■				■		■	■
A ROOM JUST FOR ME! PAGE 76		■		■					■		■	
WE'RE ON THE MOON! PAGE 77	■	■		■	■			■	■		■	

ACKNOWLEDGMENTS

Authors
Ellen Booth Church
Karen Miller

Editors
Jackie Carter
Nancy Jo Hereford
Jane Schall

Art Director
Sharon Singer

Illustrations
Nicole Rubel

Production Editors
Katie Corcoran
Rosvita Rauch

Early Childhood Division Vice President and Publisher
Helen Benham